# WOMEN, MIGRATION AND EMPIRE

# WOMEN, MIGRATION AND EMPIRE

*Edited by Joan Grant*

**tb**

**Trentham Books**

First published in 1996 by Trentham Books Limited

Trentham Books Limited
Westview House
734 London Road
Oakhill
Stoke-on-Trent
Staffordshire
England ST4 5NP

**British Cataloguing in Publication Data**
A catalogue record for this book is available from the British Library
ISBN: 1 85856 048 9

**Acknowledgements**
The editor wishes to thank the following copyright holders for permission to use manuscript material. The letter from Mary Capper is published withthe kind permission of the Society of Friends (Great Britain and Ireland Yearly Meeting). The letter from Granville Sharp is published with kind permission from the Dean and Chapter of York Minster. The Newton Papers are reproduced by kind permission of University of London Library.

Designed and typeset by Trentham Print Design Ltd., Chester and printed in Great Britain by BPC Wheatons Limited, Exeter

# Contents

# Introduction

This book evolved out of a series of discussions held by the London Feminist History Group in response to criticisms levelled at an International Women's History Conference in Amsterdam, over the lack of involvement by black and minority women. The Group held a number of discussions to examine in historical context the relationship between black and other ethnic minority women. These were issues that interested me and the idea of this book began to take shape. To my knowledge, this is the first book to link the experiences of ethnic minority women and white British women in a collaborative project.

The notion that Britain was or should remain a racially homogeneous nation is a powerful myth that historically has served to engender hostility to the successive waves of immigrants to these shores. In fact there always has been great diversity in the British population and this volume looks historically at specific immigrant communities over the past 150 years. Although the growing literature on these communities has examined the effects of racial ideology on the experiences of each group, women have tended to be absent from these accounts and this volume sets out to complete the records.

I chose the title *Women, Migration and Empire* because I wanted to link together women from minorities migrating to Britain with British women migrating to other countries, mainly within an imperial context, in all the discussions about immigration to Britain. It seems to me that the scale of the social change which post-War migration has entailed should be acknowledged on both sides. The fact is often overlooked that millions of British people were able to move to other countries, to find new opportunities. Many of these people, particularly the Scots in the aftermath of the Highland Clearances and during the early nineteenth century during the distress and unemployment that followed the Napoleonic Wars, migrated in very bitter circumstances indeed.

This volume will enable readers who are interested in Women's History to look more critically at issues of migration, Empire and British identity. It aims to do two things. Firstly to examine the experience of Black, Jewish and Irish women in Britain at times when their migration to Britain was particularly contentious: in the case of Black women in the eighteenth century, for Jewish women in 1880-1910 and for Irish women after the Famine in the 1840s. The second aim is to consider the relationship between British women and women from these communities, to see what lessons might be learnt. The first three chapters are an overview of the experiences of women from these communities during the periods mentioned above. Ann Rossiter describes the experience of Irish women in Britain in the aftermath of the Famine, Lara Marks looks at the lives of Jewish women who came to Britain in the wake of the widespread pogroms in Eastern Europe in the 1880s and my chapter looks generally at Black women in Britain during the 18th Century.

In Part 2 of the book, three chapters examine aspects of interracial interaction between women. Clare Midgely reviews the role of white British women in the Anti-Slavery movement in the 1820s and 1830s. Florence Hamilton considers the differing attitudes of British feminists to India in the 1930s and Rickie Burman discusses the interaction between women from the settled Anglo-Jewish community and the Jewish women who migrated to Britain in the 1880s.

This is not to suggest that women from different minority groups have identical histories or that racism against black people is the same as anti-semitism or anti-Irish racism. There are however, certain similarities in the experiences of women from these communities, most notably that women from all three groups came to Britain in varying degrees of unfreedom. Black women came to Britain mainly as slaves, to escape slavery; Jewish women and Irish women were fleeing, respectively, pogroms and famine.

Issues of race, migration and empire will continue to be contentious. All across Europe countries are having to come to terms with substantial minority communities. In Britain, we have seen the passing of the Asylum and Immigration Act, partly in response to the refugees fleeing from civil war in a number of countries including, most recently, Bosnia, Somalia and Kurdistan. The Chinese take-over of Hong Kong in 1997 has led to further calls for immigrations controls. The continued growth in popularity of right-wing parties across Europe is evidence that exclusion of immigrants commands widespread attention. And as always, there are sporadic calls for black people in Britain to be 'repatriated'.

It is hoped that this book will throw new light on issues of migration, Empire and British identity. Aimed at a general rather than scholarly readership, it invites a critical review of the issues, drawing upon the new ways in which history is being re-written and re-evaluated. We find ourselves in an unprecedented situation as a nation that is ethnically, racially and culturally diverse in a way that it has never been before. Our perception of the past is influenced by the present and *Women, Migration and Empire* is intended as a contribution to a process whereby we can find ways to forge a new national identity based on an appreciation of the different peoples that now inhabit this island.

During the course of preparing this volume I have become indebted to many people. I wish to thank all the contributors for preparing work for this volume and for their patience. A special thank you to Ann Rossiter for proof reading and for all her help in seeing the project to publication. I also wish to thank those who read previous drafts of my chapter, in particular Nora Harty, Helen Lowe, Delia Jarrett-Macauley, Clare Midgley and Gywneth Hughes. I would also like to thank all those who have provided encouragement and support to me while this volume has been 'in progress': Helen Lowe, Nora Harty, Madge Dresser, Rosina Visram, Julia Rosenak, Delia Jarrett-Macauley, Julia Bush, Joanna de Groot, F.J. Burford and Catherine Vaughan. I also wish to thank all those who have provided me with references and useful leads, including Ian Duffield, Chris Fyfe, James Walvin, Peter Fryer. Few women's history books are complete without a word of thanks to David Doughan at the Fawcett Library and this one is no exception. I wish to thank him for valuable research assistance. I must also mention and thank Meta Zemmick for introducing me to women's history. Finally my thanks go to all my friends and family who have helped me with this project and to thank Gillian Klein of Trentham Books for accepting the project and seeing it through to publication.

# The Contributors

**Rickie Burman** is Director of the Jewish Museum, London and was formerly the curator of the London Museum of Jewish Life. She has degrees from the Universities of Manchester and Cambridge and has researched and published on the themes of the role of women in the immigrant Jewish community.

**Joan Grant** has been an independent researcher for a number of years. Her special interest is black (African-Caribbean/African) women in Britain during the eighteenth century. She has worked in the voluntary sector and is now a solicitor.

**Florence Hamilton** is an editor in academic publishing. She recently completed a research degree on the subject of British Women and the Empire in India — 1915-1947.

**Lara Marks** is presently a lecturer at Imperial College, London. She has a doctorate from the University of Oxford, and has written numerous articles and two books on the history of ethnicity and maternal and child health. She is currently working on a book on the international history of the contraceptive pill.

**Clare Midgley** is senior lecturer in history at Staffordshire University. She has completed a doctorate on English women and the Anti-Slavery movement and written a book on the subject. She is currently editing a volume on gender and imperialism for Manchester University Press.

**Ann Rossiter** teaches Irish Studies at Luton University and the College of North West London. She has researched and published widely on questions relating to the role and status of women in Ireland. She is currently completing a doctoral thesis on Irish migrant women in Britain in contemporary times and has been active in British and Irish feminism for over two decades.

# 1

# In Search of Mary's Past:
## placing Nineteenth Century Irish immigrant women in British feminist history

*Ann Rossiter*

Oh Mary this London's a wonderful sight
With people here working by day and by night.
They don't sow potatoes, nor barley, nor wheat,
But there's gangs of them digging for gold in the streets.
At least when I axed them, that's what I was told,
So I just took a hand at this diggin' for gold,
But for all that I found there, I might as well be,
Where the Mountains of Mourne sweep down to the sea.

This ballad by Percy French, telling of the dashed hopes of an Irish
emigrant, typifies both the folk memory and the literature of nineteenth
century emigration — that it was predominantly if not exclusively a male
enterprise. It is the male immigrant who is lamenting his fate in London
and it is his wife or lover, Mary, who awaits him in Ireland. The fact that
Irish women's emigration had reached phenomenal proportions by
European standards of the time seems to have been lost on the bards and
chroniclers of the period, as much as it is ignored by their counterparts in
the late twentieth century.

Unlike in the USA and Canada where migration has been a constitutive dimension of the society, in Britain ethnicity has never been systematically recorded. Consequently Irish women in nineteenth century Britain, much as their sisters in the twentieth century, remain largely hidden from history. Although archive material exists in Britain, it is not nearly as extensive or detailed as the mass of records available in North America. This may be explained by Ireland's loss of her separate political identity following the Act of Union of 1801 and the pervasiveness of racist ideas, then as now. Considering the strong imperatives to assimilate that exist in British society, it is not surprising that second and subsequent generations of Irish origin felt impelled to deny their roots, given the derisory image associated with *Irishness*.

The recovery of women's history generally in Britain has proved an arduous business, and this is especially true of the history of working class women, whose ranks most nineteenth century Irish women joined. Historians have long claimed that it is impossible to reconstruct the lives of the so-called inarticulate, and undoubtedly leisure time and literacy, essential for the keeping of diaries and personal records, were scarce commodities amongst the women who struggled for survival at the bottom of the heap. Labour history should provide us with a rich seam of information, but not only did trade union leaders and scribes see women as undermining men's wages and unsuited to the public world of work, but they also saw their political involvement in the labour movement as a form of sub-culture unworthy of recording. This *collective amnesia* was noted very early on in the second wave of the feminist movement. In a collection of seminal writings published in 1976, Sally Alexander identified this proclivity:

> ... women's contribution to production and as well to the reproduction and maintenance of the labour force has been dismissed. This is partly because the labour and economic historians who first wrote about the working class, wrote about the organised and articulate labour move-ment — accessible through its trade union records, its news papers and the occasional autobiography.

Even in nineteenth century Dundee, widely acclaimed as a *woman's town* with its 75 per cent female workforce and with women trades unionists far outnumbering their male counterparts, William Walker (1979) was to find in the course of his researches on the labour movement there, that 'socialists of the time either chose to write poetry about the millgirl or ignore her'. He concludes:

The relative absence of reliable qualitative evidence makes recon-
struction of millgirl experience extremely difficult where the task is
not one of noting her degradation and deviancy, but of trying to
understand how her style of life had meaning for her.

For the past twenty years feminist historians have been attempting to write
a history which 'releases women from their obscurity as the wives,
mothers and daughters of working men'(Alexander,1976). There has been
a proliferation of literature about English women in the home, in the
workplace and in public life. Until very recent works appeared, the history
of Welsh and Scottish women (for example, John, 1991, Gordon and
Breitenbach, 1990) was more often than not camouflaged in the British
experience, but rarely if ever do we catch more than occasional glimpses
of Irish women. Why should this be so? In examining why women have
been rendered inconspicuous in histories of the Irish in Britain, Bronwen
Walter (1989) suggests that the lack of a strong female Irish stereotype in
nineteenth century British colloquial usage has contributed to this
deficiency in public perception. American folklore, in contrast, had
*Bridget*, the archetypal Irish domestic who, according to Diner (1983),
darted through kitchens, shattering the crockery as she went, serving as a
foil to American values and acceptable behaviour patterns. Walter points
out that in Britain collective and derogatory nouns for the Irish, such as
*Paddies and Micks* were — and are — invariably male, although she
mentions the existence of Irish women in ballad broadsheets of the time,
often referred to contemptuously as Judy (as in *Punch*), the victim of
*Paddy's* frequently violent outbursts. Walter appears to have concluded
that the references to *Biddy* encountered in the literature on the Irish in
Britain was insufficiently widespread to register as an Irish female
stereotype.

More trenchant and more commonly heard criticisms of the exclusion
of Irish women from the broader canvas of British feminist history suggest
that a deeper ideological inquiry is necessary. This should involve
questioning why feminist historians have followed the broad pattern of
socialist historiography by concentrating on the commonality of interests,
primarily class-based, and have filtered out difference, such as race,
nationality, ethnicity and religion.

The recovery of Irish women's history in Britain will necessarily be a
long and protracted enterprise, given the difficulty of obtaining primary
sources. This essay, which is derived entirely from published materials,

represents no more than a modest contribution to redressing the balance. Its purpose is to begin the task of placing Irish labouring women in British feminist history and to emphasise the contribution they made as workers to their adopted country. This follows current trends in feminist historiography which has moved from viewing women as victims, to what Gerda Lerner (1979) has called *contribution history*, an approach which emphasises women as active participants in the historical process, and is one which is echoed in *Heart of the Race: Black Women's Lives in Britain*, (Bryan, Dadzie and Scafe, 1985) where the authors argue that black women (and men):

> ... have rarely been accorded recognition for the part we have played in shaping this land. If acknowledged at all, we are usually portrayed as the passive victims of an historical necessity which began on the 'dark continent' with the Slave Trade and eventually brought us to the inner-cities of the 'Mother Country.

## The Irish presence in Britain

It is difficult to know how or why the Irish, men as well as women, could have become so easily and so quickly absorbed into the history of the British working class, as recounted by modern historians of all per-suasions, including feminists. Although Irish immigrants in nineteenth century Britain were, generally speaking, treated as an amorphous and faceless mass (a typical example being the whistling Irish servant woman who remains mostly offstage throughout Virginia Woolf's famous novel, *Mrs. Dalloway*), they were paradoxically a highly visible mass in that they were perceived as a major threat to the British way of life. The *Report of the State of the Irish Poor*, published in 1835, and probably the most detailed sociological account of the settlement of Irish immigrants during the first half of the century, describes them thus:

> The Irish emigration into Britain is an example of a less civilised population spreading themselves as a kind of substratum, beneath a more civilised community; and without excelling in any branch of industry, obtaining possession of all the lowest departments of manual labour.

Fredrich Engels, in his *Condition of the Working Class in England*, published in 1844, was no less restrained:

Wherever a district is distinguished for especial filth and especial ruinousness, the explorer may safely count upon meeting chiefly those Celtic faces which he recognises at the first glance as different from the Saxon physiognomy of the native, and the singing aspirate brogue which the true Irishman never loses.

Long before the nineteenth century, a population movement between Ireland and Britain had been recorded. Apart from the ancient Irish missionary settlements in Scotland and the North of England in the sixth century, an Irish presence was noted in Oxford as early as 1274. By the fifteenth century small Irish communities, mainly composed of merchants, existed in the principal trading ports such as Bristol, Liverpool and London. Not all Irish settlers were prosperous, however. The upheavals brought about by successive British conquests, land confiscation and plantation, rackrenting and eviction, led to a constant stream of destitute Irish roaming Britain. In response to these unwelcome visitors statutes were issued in 1413 and 1629 ordering the expulsion of Irish beggars and vagrants from Britain. There were outbursts of anti-Irish feeling in the early eighteenth century, which in 1736 developed into rioting by English harvesters against underbidding by the Irish. Another such disturbance, in Wapping and Shadwell in 1768, led to the hanging of an Irishman, James Murphy (Jackson, 1963) As the work of Irish folklorist, Anne O'Dowd, attests (O'Dowd, 191), large numbers of Irish harvesters, women as well as men, had long been migrating seasonally between the two islands in an attempt to supplement their meagre living in Ireland. Their willingness to accept low wages was more a measure of their destitution rather than any conscious attempt to violate the conventions of class solidarity. Nevertheless, the attitude of the labour movement to this reserve army of labour is made clear in a Chartist ballad (Elliot, 1930):

But work grew scarce while bread grew dear
And wages lessened too,
For Irish hordes were bidders here,
Our half-paid work to do.

The introduction of regular steam packet services between the two countries in the early 1820s further facilitated movement by providing a *floating bridge* across the Irish Sea and consequently the volume of harvest migration increased dramatically. The number of these workers is estimated at 49,911 males and 7,740 females in England and Scotland in the year 1841 (Fitzpatrick, 1989) and although farm mechanisation was to make severe inroads into the availability of seasonal work from the 1860s onwards, there were still considerable numbers crossing the Irish Sea each year, even by the turn of the century. Although a passing reference is made to Irish women in Barbara Robertson's (1990) recent feminist study of female farm workers in Scotland in the nineteenth and early twentieth centuries — which has appeared in one of the first volumes on Scottish women's history to have been published — for an affirmation of their existence and description of their working conditions one must turn to Patrick MacGill's autobiography, *Children of the Dead End,* published in 1914. MacGill, born into a family of thirteen children in Co. Donegal In 1890, and himself a potato harvester in Scotland at the age of fourteen, vividly depicts the Irish women *tatie hookers* at their daily toil:

> All day long, on their hands and knees, they dragged through the slush and rubble of the field. The baskets which they hauled after them were cased in clay to the depth of several inches and sometimes when emptied of potatoes a basket weighed over two stone ... Pools of water gathered in the hollow of the dress that covered the calves of their legs ... Two little ruts, not at all unlike the furrows left by the coulter of a skidding plough, lay behind the women in the black earth. These were made by their knees.

The living quarters provided for the potato picking squad were usually in outhouses, or sometimes in what were known as *Paddy Houses* made of brick. This arrangement, it is said, suited employer and labourer, both of whom wanted the minimum of expenditure on accommodation. MacGill describes the filth of these often rat-infested byres, the primitive cooking and washing facilities, as well as the lack of a fire to dry drenched clothing. Despite these conditions, the 10,000 or so migratory workers from County Mayo sent home postal orders amounting to more than £100,000 annually between 1876 and 1880, in advance of their return home. And a group of 425 mainly women migrants from Achill earned £5,240 (an average of £12 each) in Scotland in 1901. This income could account for up to one-third of a typical family's annual earnings (Fitzpatrick, 1989).

Apart from seasonal migration, there was also substantial permanent movement. The census of 1841 showed that there were 419,256 Irish-born in Britain, and following the Great Famine influx this rose to 727,326, reaching a peak of 806,000 in 1861. The numbers of Irish-born tended to decline for the rest of the century and the census of 1901 showed the figure to be 632,000 (O'Tuathaigh, 1985). During the Famine period and immediately after it, whole families emigrated, but subsequently the migrations were largely made up of young, single people. Precise figures for the sex ratios of emigrants first became available in the late nineteenth century, and consequently we know that of the 1,357,831 who left between 1885 and 1920, 684,159 were female; of these, 89 per cent were single and constituted a mass female movement without parallel in the history of European emigration, and what Diner (1983) refers to as a *defeminisation* of the Irish countryside.

The extent of this emigration of single Irish women, travelling alone and independently of parents or husbands, was an anomaly in the history of overall European emigration and stood in marked contrast to the custom among other European groups where women's migration was generally led and financed by male relatives. The new settlers in Britain tended to concentrate in certain urban areas, and the 1851 census showed that the population for Liverpool, for instance, contained 22.3 per cent Irish-born, for Dundee, 18.9 per cent, for Glasgow, 18.2 per cent and for London 4.6 per cent (O'Tuathaigh, 1985).

## The flight from Ireland

The nineteenth century saw huge population movements both within Europe and away from it. Figures available for the period 1815-1930 show Britain, Italy and Ireland topping the league tables of population loss due to emigration, at 11.4, 9.3 and 7.3 millions respectively (Baines, 1991). Falling mortality led to faster population growth in most of the continent which resulted in some cases in a labour surplus, even when the demands of fast-growing economies were met. Within much of Europe population shifts were from rural to urban areas, with a vast peasant army joining the ranks of the working class. Although Irish industrial development in the Belfast area absorbed some of the peasantry, the island as a whole stagnated and remained largely underdeveloped throughout the nineteenth century, and large numbers were pushed out through unemployment, the pressures of poverty and famine. An Irish proletariat was also born in this period, but its contribution was primarily to the factories and mills of Britain, America and the Antipodes in the absence of an industrial revolution at home.

Ireland suffered its greatest population loss during the Great Famine of 1845-9 when about two million died of starvation and famine-related diseases and one and a half million emigrated. The immediate reason for the tragedy was a blight which attacked several million acres of potato crop on which much of the peasantry depended. In a very short time many were left in a wretched state. At the height of the catastrophe, the Reverend S. Godolplin Osbourne, while on a tour of Limerick, was overwhelmed by the dirt, disorder and decay (Gallagher, 1982):

> Every street was dilapidated, dark, hideous, filled with a ragged swarm of humanity. Stark eyes stared out of the dirty windows, frail children paddled up and down the broken steps around their soiled and unkempt mothers, whose careworn and frightened looks told of the continual worry over how to feed them ... The men, pale and gaunt, their eyes wild and hollow, and their gait feeble, threadbare garments hanging from their bodies.

Although the majority of the people depended heavily on a potato diet because they lacked the financial means to do otherwise, three-quarters of Ireland's cultivatable land was under cereals — wheat, oats, barley and corn — almost all being shipped to England. The cattle and sheep which grazed in Ireland, and the pigs fed, were likewise not eaten but sent to Britain for consumption. The Irish peasantry, which accounted for roughly six million of the country's population of eight million, subsisted on the potato and grew cereals and engaged in mixed agriculture to pay the rent to the several thousand landlords, descendants of English or Scots mercenaries and adventurers. Some of these were settled in Ireland, but the vast majority (probably 70 per cent) resided in Britain and were known as *absentees*. With its high nutritional levels, no crop other than the potato could have borne the burden of feeding so many people on so little arable land.

For the Irish, the responsibility for the famine lay entirely with the landlords and the British administration, and their term for it, the *Great Starvation*, is evidence of this. British politicians, economists and observers in contrast interpreted the tragedy entirely in Malthusian terms and as a punishment for Ireland's demographic profligacy, since the population had doubled in the period 1785-1841 from an estimated 4 million to 8.2 million. Even before the famine occurred Thomas Carlyle, the English novelist, had issued this warning cry (Mokyr, 1983):

> This cannot last, Heaven disowns it. Earth is against it; Ireland will be burnt into a black unpeopled field of ashes that this should last ... The time has come when the Irish population must be improved a little or exterminated.

It has to be said, however, that the Irish peasantry were locked into a subsistence economy with no control over the means of production and lacked the means and possibly the will to make rational long-term decisions about population size. Catholicism is frequently cited as the reason for large families, but as discussed later in this chapter, in the absence of contraception continuous childbearing was the fate of most women, not only in Ireland but in Britain too, until well into the twentieth century. A more likely explanation lay in the fact that landlords had earlier taken advantage of the increased demand for cereals on the British market, stemming from growing industrialisation and the exigencies of the Napoleonic wars, and adopted a system of production in Ireland which stimulated population growth.

Between 1770 and 1810 the price of corn had doubled and, in order to benefit, landlords had to choose between growing the crop themselves with the use of hired labour, or renting out plots to peasant farmers who could utilise family labour. The latter option was the one adopted as the least troublesome. This system of agricultural production allowed for sub-division and relatively early marriage. A large family was valued for the labour it provided, since cereal production was labour intensive, and it also promised security in old age. The British administration in Ireland failed to institute a Poor Law until 1838, and even then it was very restrictive, with the result that children tended to be viewed by parents as their sole insurance against old age.

Population growth was inevitable under this system, and in the decades preceding the famine the strains of sub-division were only too visible, with dwarf-sized plots sustaining an impoverished peasantry, forced to live off a diet of potatoes in order to pay the rent. Only the textile cottage industries and seasonal and long term migration eased a potentially explosive situation, especially when the Corn Laws which protected British and Irish cereals from cheap foreign imports were repealed in 1846. Coinciding with the disaster faced by Irish cereal growers as foreign grain flooded the British market, was the advent of the potato blight which brought the fragile Irish agricultural economy to its knees almost overnight.

The famine provided the opportunity for landlords to adopt more capitalist methods of farming and to turn over their land from cereal production to cattle rearing to meet the latest needs of the British market following the demise of the Corn Laws. Marx's fatalistic prediction that it was Ireland's national destiny to become 'an English sheepwalk and cattle pasture, her people banished by sheep and ox', was fast becoming a reality. As with the Highland Clearances in Scotland, landlords seized their chance to rid estates of surplus tenants and thousands of evictions took place, ostensibly because of failure to pay rent.

It also became a condition of obtaining public relief that tenants relinquish any claim on their land, and in some cases, landlords offered assisted passage to those willing to emigrate. Lord Palmerston, for instance, sent 2,000 people to America in nine ships. The object of assisted passage was to rid the estates of the worst and to retain the best; the selection for emigration were thus the poorest, the weakest and the most unskilled and untrained. Women and young girls frequently fell into this category and were selected as servants (and sometimes wives) for the Americas and the colonies. Those who were unassisted, and unable to afford the fare to North America, crossed the Irish Sea to Britain, many hoping to earn their passage money to the 'New World' after a short period of residence. Engels was not alone in his ironic characterisation of these Hibernian hordes:

> (who) migrate for fourpence to England, on the deck of a steamship on which they are often packed like cattle, (and) insinuate themselves everywhere. The worst dwellings are good enough for them; their clothing causes them little trouble, so long as it holds together by a single thread; shoes they know not; their food consists of potatoes and potatoes only; whatever they earn beyond these needs they spend upon drink. What does such a race want with high wages?

Nearly all classes suffered a devastating blow from the famine, including British landlords, many of whom were bankrupted. Irish society experienced a severe psychological shock, paving the way for many changes, some of which have endured until the late twentieth century. Apart from the massive loss of population from death, and a high emigration rate which has persisted even in modern times, a transformed rural class structure, single inheritance, rising age at marriage, declining marriage and birth rates, and a stagnant death rate, became marked features of post-Famine society. The size of the labouring and small farming classes dropped dramatically, while land consolidation gave rise to a category of Irish farmers owning middle and large sized farms, who showed themselves as amenable to capitalist methods in agricultural production and to the levying of as exorbitant rents as the British landlords they displaced.

The Irish people became subordinated to the land as population growth was curbed, not by limiting family size, but through the establishment of severe impediments in the way of marriage and the formation of families. From being a relatively early marrying population, they became a late and rare marrying one. Between 1845 and 1914 the average male age at marriage rose from 25 to 33, and the average female age from about 21 to 28. The number of marriages dropped dramatically and large numbers failed to marry at all. (Lee, 1973) Inheritance patterns changed from sub-division to the most favoured son acquiring the land, and often only in later years, in an attempt to control population growth.

Women's status in the farming communities received a serious blow. Firstly, the move from the more labour intensive cereals to cattle rearing, primarily a male-dominated activity in Ireland as it has been in many other societies, meant that women were marginalised in agricultural production. Secondly, while the impact of the British Industrial Revolution was felt by both men and women in the cottage textile industries in Ireland, the consequences for women were more severe. Mary E. Daly (1981) points out that manufacturing industry employed a mere 17 per cent of the Irish work force in 1891 as compared with 27 per cent in 1841, the brunt of the decline being borne by women workers. This was primarily because of the volume of women in the trade and the very limited openings available elsewhere. Also of significance was women's loss of the status they previously enjoyed as wives and potential marriage partners, as their ability to contribute to the family's income was now undermined. (Lee, 1978).

Except in the Belfast area where they formed a large proportion of the workforce in the textile mills, Irish women were relegated to domestic service as their main source of waged work. Dowries became imperative for virtually all classes, making love matches a thing of the past. From the Famine period onwards until well into the twentieth century, it was common for only one daughter of the family to enter the state of matrimony due to the size of dowry being demanded, despite the fact that marriage and motherhood increasingly became the only occupation open to many Irish women. It is not surprising therefore that they emigrated in such numbers in search of work, status and an unfettered marriage system.

## Irish women's world of work — a story in fragments

The majority of permanent Irish immigrants in Britain were concentrated in the ranks of the semi-skilled, unskilled and casual labour force, in construction, railway building, transportation, dockside labour, food distribution, cotton manufacturing, the clothing trade and domestic service. The traditional view, that seasonal workers provided a pool of cheap labour and thereby undermined workers' living standards generally, also extended to those who took up long-term residence.

Although it is the subject of some controversy, it would seem on the basis of the empirical evidence available that the Irish had a considerable impact at all stages of Britain's industrial revolution (see Williamson, 1986 and Hunt, 1981). Handley's (1970) account of navvying in Scotland, for instance, shows that the Irish presence was significant in digging the 3,000 miles of canals, and later the railways constructed across Britain in order to diminish the prohibitive cost of moving goods overland. Besides digging the canals, navvies also built huge drainage systems for the new industries and the towns which grew around them, as well as reservoirs, roads, bridges, docks and harbours. The *navvy* (an abbreviation of navigator), was a labourer who cut the *navigation* and has been viewed traditionally as a footloose male, inured to a life of wandering from one job to the next, and for a miserable wage. Handley found evidence, however, of Irish men being accompanied by their wives and families, who were subjected to all the deprivation such an itinerant existence brought.

The Irish were cheap, mobile and industrious, and since most were in their late teens and early twenties, the host society benefited from acquiring a labour force of *instant adults*. They would also appear to be less fastidious than the native-born. Sifting through published material on women's economic activity in Britain, where it is only possible to gain some glimpses of Irish women's world of work, we find, for instance, that settled Irish women continued the tradition of field labour, established through seasonal migration. Frances Finnegan (1985), in her study of the Irish in nineteenth century York, found that Irish women accounted for all female field labourers and for almost 80 per cent of the general female labourers as recorded in the 1851 Census. Even when these agricultural labourers became permanent urban settlers, they often continued to go out to nearby country areas in the summertime to take advantage of harvest work.

Irish women also appear to have been occupied in the traditional male areas of mining and smelting, and as such challenged the dominant ideals of femininity. For instance, David Fitzpatrick (1989) discovered, when investigating reports from Poor Law inspectors, that by 1870 Kerry women who had been seasonal migrants regularly worked in the iron furnaces of South Wales in the springtime after their work in potato planting was over. It is interesting to note that in the first volume devoted to an historical examination of Victorian and early twentieth century women in Wales, and one which adopts a feminist perspective (see John, 1991), no reference to these or other immigrant Irish women appears. Angela John (1984), however, in a footnote to her account of nineteenth century women coalminers in the Wigan area of Lancashire, refers to an influx of Irish pit girls to the coalfields in the vicinity in the 1860s, but we learn nothing specific about them, their numbers, where they came from, or why, although at least one living former pit worker with an Irish surname — Jane Carroll — features in the account. It may be, for instance, that these were women who had worked the ore mines of Cork, Kerry, Limerick, Wexford and Waterford but were forced to migrate to England and the United States when cheap American ore began to flood the British and Irish markets in the 1860s and 70s. (Cowman, 1983)

The Irish contribution to the manufacturing of textiles was also considerable. Eric Hobsbawm (1968) estimates that in the first stage, roughly from the late eighteenth to mid-nineteenth century, capital accumulation in any one industry on the basis of low wage labour was sufficient to generate a further expansion without recourse to capital finance from elsewhere. Added to this, some Irish workers brought with them skills acquired in the textile industry in Ireland, which they transferred to the British setting. The Irish — men, women and children — flocked to the cotton towns of Bradford, Blackburn, Bolton, Burnley, Oldham, Preston, Rochdale, Wigan, and to the twin cities of Manchester and Salford, the hub of the industry. By 1851, the census figures show that 13.1 per cent of the population of Manchester and Salford were Irish-born (O'Tuathaigh, 1985), and this figure does not include children born of Irish parents, since ethnicity was not recorded. Wigan had the greatest concentration of Irish-born inhabitants in England, large numbers being employed in the less skilled spinning processes. In the Lancashire cotton industry women had more equality with men than in most other industries and were to be found as combers, carders, warpers, weavers and ring spinners. They were excluded only from mule spinning, a resolutely all-male craft, and from being tacklers or supervisors. Despite their numbers and status as workers, it is interesting that no study of Irish women textile operatives in this region appears to be have been published.

Lobban's study of Greenock in Scotland (1971) finds that 44.3 per cent of the female workers in the textile mills in 1851 were from Ulster, where they had obtained their skills. Dundee, already an established linen-weaving centre in the 1820s, and with a jute-manufacturing industry by the 1840s, became the main area in Britain for the production of coarse linen. Eleanor Gordon's (1987) work on Dundee's women jute workers in the period 1870-1906, although not alluding to ethnic origin, states that the demand for cheap female labour was such that the city became a town of migrant labour, drawing a workforce from the surrounding countryside, the Highlands and Ireland. By 1851 a 19 per cent Irish population was recorded, many of whom had left Ireland in family groups when the industry declined there during the Great Famine years, and following a tradition already established in the 1820s and 1830s. Brenda Collins (1981), whose work is specifically on the Irish, establishes that Dundee was an obvious choice for families because the pattern of the cottage linen industry, established in Ireland and involving all family members, was able to be retained there until well into the 1860s. The Paisley textile manufactures also benefited from this system of working, as did Midland silk manufacturers. Mr Taylor, proprietor of Newton Heath silk mill near Manchester, attested in the *Report on the State of the Irish Poor in Great Britain*, published in 1835, that:

> The moment I have a turn-out, and am fast for hands, I send for ten, fifteen or twenty families as the case may be. I usually send to Connaught, and I get the children, chiefly girls of farmers and cottiers. The whole family comes, father, mother and children. I provide them with no money. I suppose they sell up what they have, walk to Dublin, pay their passage to Liverpool and come to Manchester by rail or walk it. The communications are generally made through the parties in my employ.

Unlike the linen sector, there is little evidence of a family economy in the jute industry of Dundee. The industry depended heavily on cheap female labour and attracted large numbers of single Irish women textile workers in their teens and early twenties, some from settled families, but also many who emigrated in sibling groups. Eleanor Gordon states that the city had the highest percentage of married women working in Scotland, that in the jute industry about one third of the female labour force over twenty was married, and that the largest single category of workers was women aged between twenty-five and forty-five. Doubtless, this category included Irish women.

Of all the areas of Irish settlement London is one of the best documented. Nineteenth century London provided no single staple form of employment for women on the scale of the northern textile towns. It was a city of both skilled trades in ship-building and engineering, and small workshops from which semi-skilled and unskilled workers produced a wide variety of goods. Sally Alexander's (1976) feminist study of London women's work in the period 1820-50 provides a detailed analysis of the variety of female occupations, but unfortunately, does not refer to the subjects' ethnicity. We are therefore particularly indebted to Henry Mayhew, the social investigator whose work was first published in 1851, for his vivid accounts of immigrant life in the metropolis. He identified street selling as a major occupation for Irish men, women and children and estimated that, in mid-century, at least 10,000 made their living by hawking in various parts of London, about three-quarters of them selling fruit. This is his depiction of an early morning scene at Covent Garden market:

> Groups of apple-women, with strawpads on their crushed bonnets, and coarse shawls, crossing their bosoms, sit on their porters' knots, chatting in Irish, and smoking short pipes; every passer-by is hailed with the cry of, 'Want a baskit, yer honor?

After Mayhew, the first study conducted which treats Irish women in London with more than a passing reference is that of Lynn Hollen Lees (1979), an American academic. Her work is in the tradition of American urban history and sociology and is concerned with the creation, organisation and affirmation of Irish ethnicity in five areas of Victorian London. She records that Irish women entered the metropolitan economy with difficulty. They were to be found in the clothing trades, needlework being the principal skilled occupation. Lees also found evidence of them in semi-skilled areas such as the making of artificial flowers, lint scraping, fur pulling and the finishing of manufactured goods, such as hats and umbrellas. Subsidiary tasks in the leather, clothing and paper industries were also carried out by them. Their primary occupation, however, was domestic service.

Domestic service was given as the occupation of 93.3 per cent of all women leaving Ireland for all destinations, including Britain and the USA, in the period 1877-1880; between 1881 and 1890 the figure was 95.7 per cent, and between 1891 and 1900 it was 94.6 per cent. (Jackson, 1963) It is therefore not surprising to find that the dominant part played by domestic service in the working lives of Irish women in Britain is highlighted in virtually all the studies of Irish settlement in Britain. James Treble's (1986) work on the female unskilled labour market in Glasgow states that Irish women were substantially over-represented in two of the main areas of casual domestic employment, namely, chars and laundry workers. Similarly, David Large's (1985) research on the Irish in Bristol in the census year of 1851 shows that the vast majority employed in domestic service described themselves as *general servant or maid of all work, and never as lady's maid or parlour maid.* These and other sources would suggest that Irish women were considered unsuitable for work which brought them into close contact with their employers.

Studies on domestic service in nineteenth century Britain from a feminist perspective by Theresa McBride (1976), Pamela Horn (1975), and Lynn Jamieson's (1990) work specifically on Scotland, all commit the Irish to obscurity. The same pattern of omission extends throughout a very considerable feminist literature on the nineteenth century family which also encompasses a discussion of the role of domestic servants. This literature provides us with a very cogent analysis of the bourgeois family model of the last century, with its ethos of the correct ordering of domestic life, reflecting and reinforcing bourgeois ideas of society generally. In this scheme of things, men and women had their separate spheres, a mirror image of the necessary separation between working and middle classes. Maintaining this separation and a veneer of respectability, according to Davidoff, L'Esperance and Newby (1976), became an obsession with all strata of the nineteenth century middle classes, and:

> ... meant a constant urge to live beyond the means of the household and to make up the difference by exploiting the labour of the most subordinate members, i.e. young servants, children, unmarried daughters and in lesser households, wives. The cash worth of such labour was played down ... But the fact that the ideal, if it was ever attempted, depended on hard, unremitting drudgery performed by often lonely, tired out young maid servants secreted away in underground basements, sleeping in freezing attics, carrying hods of

coals and heavy toddlers from early morning to late at night was not allowed to intrude on the dream.

Rarely is it ever mentioned that a significant proportion of middle-class households in straitened circumstances, particularly in London and the bigger cities, hired what was considered the least desirable, and hence the cheapest, form of labour — the Irish serving girl. Patricia Branca (1975) estimates that at the £300 yearly income level (the bulk of middle class in nineteenth century Britain earned this or less) only a maid-of-all-work, whose wage was between £9-14 a year, could be employed, along with an occasional girl. Such domestics were the means by which the families of tradesmen and clerks achieved *gentility* and as such played a major role in the establishment of status for a growing British middle class in the second half of the nineteenth century.

Unlike the situation in the United States where there was continual demand, Irish women faced serious competition in domestic work in Britain. Throughout the century there was an over-supply of unskilled female labour, so that between 1830 and 1855 approximately one in every six English women was employed as a domestic, their numbers growing until the 1880s and then beginning to decline. The typical British servant, Patricia Branca tells us, was badly trained, having come from a background of extreme poverty in the countryside or the city slum. She had no experience of what the middle class considered *civilised* behaviour, such as cleanliness, honesty and sobriety and she was generally very young. Employers' dissatisfaction and servants' distaste for the long hours of work, miserable accommodation, loss of freedom and degrading master-servant relations ensured a high turnover rate in this line of work. A survey reported in Parliamentary Papers of 1899 found, for instance, that 47 per cent of a sample of over 2,400 servants had been in the same household for less than a year.

Theresa McBride found that a substantial segment of the servant class was downwardly mobile and ended up begging or in prostitution. If this was the fate of many British servants, what then of Irish domestics who were held in much less esteem? Lynn Hollen Lees reports that Irish servants had a reputation in the metropolis for being *saucy and incompetent* and although they were willing to take up the less desirable posts, where they were paid only one or two shillings a week plus board, it was common for them to quit or be fired. She cites London priests issuing warnings in the *Catholic Standard* during the 1850s that prostitution or begging might well be the fate of Irish girls thinking of crossing the water to go 'in service'. However, by the end of the nineteenth century domestic service was fast developing outside the realm of the family, in institutions such as hospitals and in businesses, for instance. How Irish women fared in this type of service remains to be uncovered by future researchers.

We get a rare impressions of an Irish girl's lot in a British household of limited means from *Bridget Kiernan*, a short story by the Anglo-Irish novelist, Norah Hoult, published in 1928. The eponymous Bridget is depicted as a young, careless Irish servant, constantly taunted by the lady of the house, who perceives her as dirty and uncouth. Hoult claimed the story was 'created from life', based on her observations of a household in which she was staying.

> Leaving instructions, Mrs Fitzroy went away to get dressed in a spirit of acute dissatisfaction. It was a reflection on the house, she thought, to have such an untidy depressed-looking girl about as Bridget. And Irish people were supposed to be bright and witty! Sooner or later she'd have to give her notice, and start the search all over again. Or move into a flat with a gas stove, and manage herself with a day girl. This servant problem was really driving responsible women like herself mad.

## Married women and work

Hasia Diner (1983), citing evidence from a number of different surveys conducted in nineteenth century America, suggests that once they married, Irish women virtually withdrew from the labour market. She quotes from one which emphasised the centrality of the married woman's role as homemaker, which:

> husband and children alike bent every effort to maintain her in it. In consequence the Irish family had a unity and dignity which neither poverty nor prosperity could destroy.

Diner also suggests that working-class Irish women in America stood in marked contrast to other groups in their withdrawal from the labour force but also in their aversion to homework, unlike Eastern European Jewish women who were engaged in sweatshop labour in their homes making garments, or Italian women who made artificial flowers and buttons. In her researches Diner encountered references to married Irish women taking in laundry, a money-earning activity also common amongst Irish women in Britain, as was the taking in of lodgers.

Diner identifies the Catholic Church with its emphasis on motherhood and domesticity, as the cause of Irish women's abandonment of work outside the home. While not dismissing the influence of the Church, a number of factors have to be taken into account when considering married women and paid work generally in the century. Joan Scott and Louise Tilly, in their pathbreaking work published in 1975, emphasised the extent of confusion that has existed in this area, stressing that historians have generally assumed that women at home in any time period have been non-productive, the antithesis of women at work. As if to bear out this assertion, we find that only 22 per cent of married Irish women in London are listed in the 1851 Census as occupied. However, a study by Catherine Hakim (1980) of the nineteenth century censuses and their assumptions regarding the economic activity of family members, suggests that married women's paid work tended to fluctuate with the ages of their children or with the changing fortunes of the main breadwinner, for example, during illness or unemployment. Women regularly found intermittent and seasonal alternatives to full-time jobs which they would not necessarily regard as formal *employment* when making declarations to the census taker. In fact, there are several references in the literature to Irish women and their children leaving the city each year to go hop-picking in Kent, and for short periods of fruit-picking or general work in the fields. Battersea laundries were staffed by gas workers' wives in the summmmer and builders' wives in winter when the men were laid off, and doubtless there were Irish women amongst them. Occasional piece work taken into the home also ensured the survival of the family at difficult times, much as did hawking.

Open-air food selling is a female domain in many cultures and has a long tradition amongst Irish women, immortalised in the song, *Molly Malone*, about the Dublin shellfish-seller who 'wheeled her wheelbarrow through streets, broad and narrow'. It is also one which is still very much alive today in and around Dublin's Moore Street and Henry Street. The sheer inventiveness and survival strategies of the women, some of them married, described in *Maggie Feathers and Missie Reilly: Hawking Life in Dublin's City Quay* (Bennett, 1984), a piece of oral history about late nineteenth and early twentieth century street-sellers, are impressive:

The Reilly work day began at dawn with skin scavenging. The 'skins' were once a moderately prominent feature of the Dublin scene. One of Leopold Bloom's early jaunts in Ulysses took him through Lime Street to where 'by Brady's cottages a boy for the skins lolled, his bucket of offal linked, smoking a chewed fagbutt.' Laughing as this is read to her, Maggie Reilly reacts: 'That must have been one of ours', for the Reillys collected skins at Brady's cottages and all over the area Bloom was traversing. Skins were a feature because some Dubliners kept pigs. 'Skins' were potato and turnip peelings, but also stale bread or anything at all from the wide world of what pigs will eat. Many householders happily donated to the porcine cause in order to eliminate problems of rotting refuse.

These instances, together with the snatches we pick up from Mayhew's accounts of Irish women in the London scene, as well as Lees' researches, tend to indicate that married Irish women participated in the labour market to a far greater extent than allowed for in Diner's version. There is also a failure to emphasise that a marriage bar frequently operated in domestic service, the area in which most Irish women were occupied. Lara Marks (1990), a British feminist researcher, whose contribution on Irish and Jewish married women in the East End of London is a rare if not unique focus on ethnic minorities, while underscoring the different cultural attitudes to married women's work in the two communities, is at pains to highlight a tradition of paid labour amongst Irish women. It also needs to be stressed that Irish women brought with them to their new homeland a culture of work, from their involvement in the family farm and the cottage industries which extended beyond domestic and childcare responsibilities.

The only research encountered by this writer which would sustain the working class *captive housewife* phenomenon is Pat Ayers and Jan Lambertz's (1986) study of domestic violence in working-class Liverpool families in the early part of the twentieth century. Although the study fails to identify the ethnic origins of its subjects — the wives and families of Liverpool dockworkers — it is probably safe to assume that many were Irish and possibly Catholics. From it we learn that wives had to resort to all sorts of devious strategies in the use of credit or the earning of a copper 'on the side' to bolster their husbands' image of themselves as sole breadwinners, even though dock work was a notoriously unstable occupation. It has to be remembered that by the early twentieth century, the period which the study covers, the ideal of the *family wage*, earned exclusively by the man as head of the household, had penetrated to the lowest sections of the working class. This was reinforced by the trade union movement, civil servants (notably those responsible for health and social welfare), and the churches, Protestant as well as Catholic.

Comparisons with women of other ethnic groups are also difficult to make without some knowledge of family circumstances. For instance, Irish immigrant families tended to be nuclear in form, and, with the exception of the Famine diaspora when whole families left Ireland, an extended family network may not have been on tap to care for small children while mothers were out at work. Looking after babies and young children involved relentless physical labour, added to which there was constant illness due to infectious diseases and childhood complaints. From available statistics it is estimated that 75-85 per cent of working class London women breast-fed their babies. A study carried out in Paddington in 1904 found that 77 per cent were breastfeeding and another in St. Pancras in the same year ascertained that 82 per cent of infants were wholly breast-fed in the first three months and another 10 per cent partially. Ellen Ross (1986), looking at London's working class mothers in the period 1870 to 1918, says:

> Even if viewed narrowly as a biological event motherhood was all-encompassing. Childbearing among the poor began soon after marriage and continued into middle age. Figures for England as a whole show that in the cohort of women who married in about 1860 63% had five children or more; only 12.3% of the women married in 1925 had this many children. The 1911 Fertility Census found that almost 20% of women who had completed their childbearing by that year had eight or more children. Continuous childbearing, however, had become the fate only of poor women, as the middle classes had begun in the 1850s or so to have smaller families.

Housework was also an arduous business, especially in the tenements of the inner city and it was not unusual for older girls to be kept home from school to help with the chores, and also to look after babies and small children. Not only was truancy common among girls, but older boys were also expected to find work to supplement the meagre wages of a labouring father — frequently less than £1 a week, even in the early twentieth century. Even for women textile workers in Northern England and Scotland who earned relatively good wages and could afford to pay childminders, the burden of work carried by married women in the trade was colossal. Elizabeth Roberts (1984) quotes oral evidence from a Lancashire textile worker who complained:

> ... when I had the baby I went right back to work because I had to do for the money ... I would be washing at 1 o'clock in the morning and getting up at 5 o'clock to go to work.

Roberts records that considerable numbers of married women gave up full-time work as soon as the family's financial circumstances permitted, regardless of religion or ethnic background. However, it is important to stress that there were wide geographical differences in the percentages of married women in work, especially full-time work in Britain. In a later publication, Roberts (1988) establishes that towns such as Blackburn, Burnley, Hinkley, and the City of London had 40 per cent of married women in full-time work in 1911, while Barrow-in-Furness and York had ten per cent or less. She demonstrates that towns where a relatively large number of married women worked were also areas where high percentages of unmarried women were also occupied, thus reflecting the generally more favourable state of the local female labour market.

We might therefore infer that consideration of these and other factors is important when drawing general conclusions on the work patterns of minority women. Given that research on Irish women in Britain is still in its infancy and much primary source material has yet to be located, it is important for researchers to be aware of the stereotypes and *cultural frame* into which an ethnic group can fall, sometimes due to myths of its own making but, more often than not, due to the sheer weight of prejudice in the host community.

## Nationality, Ethnicity, and Religion

Life in nineteenth century Britain was for the Irish a harsh and disorientating experience. Apart from their reputation for undermining material standards by the acceptance of lower wages, they were seen as a threat to the British way of life, distinguishable from the native population by race, religion and nationality. Their intense poverty caused them to be widely regarded as the harbingers of crime and disorder, and consequently they often fell foul of the law, being five times more likely to be convicted and imprisoned than their British counterparts, especially where petty crime was involved. Portia Robinson (1988) records that in the years 1789-1828 at least half of the transported women in Botany Bay, the British penal settlement of New South Wales, had been born in Ireland. Of these at least ten per cent were convicted in England, and this figure may have been even higher, for native-place was not invariably recorded in trials conducted in Britain.

Hostility to this alien group also took a racist form. The pseudo-scientific theories of race propounded by Victorian anthropologists and ethnologists which gained common currency through popular literature, included the Irish. In this scheme of things, 'races' were said to have inherited differences not only of physique but also of character, and were placed in a hierarchical scale of measurement where Anglo-Saxons were to be found at the top, black people at the bottom, and Celts and Jews somewhere in between. The object of the exercise was not only to prove English superiority but, inevitably, the unsuitability of the 'inferior' races for self-government. A study by the American writer L.P. Curtis highlights the efforts made throughout the Victorian era to prove that the English and the Irish were separated by clear-cut racial as well as religious and cultural barriers. Physiognomical differentiation was central to this endeavour, and men of letters invested considerable energy in measuring the cranium, facial angles, thickness of the lips, size of jaw and levels of pigmentation to provide a scientific basis for their claim. The *bulging forward of the lower part of the face, the chin more or less retreating, the large mouth and thick lips, they deduced, indicated a quickness in perception, but a deficiency in reasoning power.*

Much anti-Irish feeling was exacerbated by deep religious animosity towards Catholicism, which the majority of the immigrants espoused. In nineteenth century Britain religious affiliation persisted as an important source of a person's identity, not a mere mask for other identifications, such as class. Anti-Catholicism fabricated its own world vision and a demonology in which the horrors of the Inquisition and the corruption and intrigues of the Catholic Church were frustrated only by the activities and ideology of Protestantism. Since the Reformation, restrictions on Catholics had been severe and it was not until 1836 that an Act of Parliament was passed allowing Catholic chapels licences to marry. By mid-century the election of Catholics to office in the boroughs became possible and prohibitions on Catholic education were relaxed. Finally, in 1850 the Catholic hierarchy was restored in England and Wales (in Scotland this was delayed until 1874), but this had the effect of stirring the old and latent fears about Catholic loyalty to the Crown and did much to fuel the flames of militant anti-Catholicism. The *Times* commented in 1853:

We very much doubt whether in England, or indeed in any free Protestant country, a true Papist can be a good subject. But if all this had been avowed some years ago, the opportunities of Popery would never have been what they are.

Anti-Catholic agitation, hitherto fairly commonplace but mainly non-violent, began to break out into serious rioting, notably at Stockport in 1852, Oldham in 1861, London in 1862 and for the duration of the more widespread Murphy disturbances of 1867-71. It was, as Graham Davis (1991) stresses, a tragic coincidence that growing public concern about acute urban problems occurred at the same time as the rising tide of Irish immigration into the cities of mainland Britain. The Irish, he says,

> became a target for denunciation by reformers and officials alike. As numerous investigations and commissions of inquiry revealed the alarming scale of urban squalor, crime, drunkenness and epidemic disease, an explanation was found in the presence of an alien people. The horrific details uncovered were in truth part of an old problem. Slums had existed long before in London and elsewhere but the problems were now perceived to be of epic proportions. The burgeoning cities lacked the administrative and legislative capacities to deal with the crisis and even if they had been in place, there was no recognition in contemporary understanding of the economic forces that created a slum district. ... the association between Irish immigrants and slum conditions became established in a crisis atmosphere.

Given this level of animosity and division it is astonishing that urban histories of Britain in the modern period have failed to refer to the question of ethnicity until the arrival of African-Caribbean and Asian workers in the post-second World War period began to be documented. Grappling with the reasons for the omission of the Irish, Joan Smith (1986) argues that this is a consequence of the complete disagreement, in the field of both race relations and of historical research, about how far the Irish in Britain were an ethnic minority in the nineteenth century. At the heart of this disagreement, she says, is an absence of discussion on the role of ethnicity, a factor which was crucial in designating the Irish as the alien *other*. The long colonial relationship between Britain and Ireland resulted in the Irish being stigmatised as an inferior people which, coupled with religious prejudice and the denial of access to wealth, power and status, led them to affirming their own identity. Smith argues that John Rex's highly influential theory on the construction of ethnic minorities in Britain constantly seeks to emphasise the overarching importance of skin colour in the construction of prejudice and she emphasises that while acknowledging the partial colonial status of the Irish, Rex dismisses the Irish experience as being not at all comparable to contemporary race relations problems.

Equally, the historian Sheridan Gilley (1978), in an essay on the Irish experience in Britain, has dismissed L.P. Curtis' argument that anti-Black racism in the United States compared with English dislike of the Victorian Irish. Because there was no difference in skin colour, he argues, 'it was the Irish rejection of English values which — rather than race — aroused English dislike of them'. For Gilley to be convinced that racism existed, there would have to have been what he terms 'anti-Celtic' racism on the part of the British rather than 'non-racial resentments' cloaked in the terminology of race.

Given the reluctance of sociologists and historians such as Rex and Gilley to acknowledge that the nineteenth century Irish were ghettoised in the job market and in the housing market, that they were discriminated against politically and racially, and were confronted by a hostile majority, it is not surprising that they have come to be seen as a form of sub-proletarian class which was quickly absorbed into the mainstream of British working class life in the second and third generations, and hence rendered invisible. Rex (1980) confirms this belief in his essay on immigrants and British labour:

> So far as Britain is concerned it may be said that its ethnic composition is astonishingly homogeneous, but its class formations are strongly developed ... Amongst the working classes, there has, of course, been continuous immigration since the beginnings of the industrial revolution, but it has been overwhelmingly the immigration of an ethnically very similar group, namely the Irish ... The closeness of Irish and British culture has made incorporation of the Irish into the working class relatively easy. Usually within three generations Irish families were able to move into core working-class positions and beyond them.

In a wry essay which examines his own marginalisation as an Ulster socialist and labour historian in the British Left, James Young (1987) argues that 'inside the world of *British* socialist historiography, the word British simply meant English' and that the cultural traditions of the Left in Britain between 1880 and 1980 developed within the framework of English imperialism. This has meant that the Celts — the Scots, the Welsh and the Irish — were seen as forming a marginal component of the working class and a subordinate element of the British workers' movement. It has taken, he says, the revived imperialism of the Thatcherite era and the accelerated break-up of Britain to stimulate English socialist historians to analyse their own history and attitudes more critically than ever before.

Given this legacy of historiography inherited by British feminists whose ideological persuasion has traditionally been of the Left, it is hardly surprising that women of the *Celtic fringe* have been rendered more or less invisible in their work. However, as Sheila Rowbotham (1989) argues, feminist searchers, academic or otherwise, have above all been concerned to turn male-defined priorities and ordered intellectual definitions upside down and to place the personal at the heart of their politics. Given this equally dominant tradition and the fact that a new generation of young searchers schooled in a multi-ethnic Britain are now writing, we must be aware, as Ante Ciliga, a left dissident in the early days of the Russian Revolution observed, that the thought of the past can prevent us 'from battering down open doors'.

## Acknowledgements

I would like to thank Anna Davin, Rayah Feldman and Jutta Schwarzkopf for reading this essay and making many helpful comments. My special thanks to Gautam Appa for all his support, especially with the bibliography, and to Meera Appa for her forebearance while this project was under way.

## References

Ayers, P., and Lambertz, J. (1986) 'Marriage Relations, Money, and Domestic Violence in Working Class Liverpool, 1919-39', Lewis, J. (ed.), *Labour and Love: Women's Experience of Home and Family, 1850-1940*, Oxford, Basil Blackwell.

Alexander, S. (1976) 'Women's Work in Nineteenth-Century London; A Study of the Years 1820-50', Mitchel, J and Oakley, A, (eds.), *The Rights and Wrongs of Women*, Harmondsworth, Penguin.

Baines, D. (1991) *Emigration from Europe, 1815-1930*, Studies in Economic and Social History, London, Macmillan.

Bennett, D. (1984), 'Maggie Feathers and Missie Reilly: Hawking in Dublin's City Quay', Curtin, C, Kelly, M, and O'Dowd, L. (eds.), *Culture and Ideology in Ireland*, Galway, Galway University Press.

Branca, P. (1975) *Silent Sisterhood: Middle Class Women in the Victorian Home*, London, Croom Helm.

Bryan, B., Dadzie, S and Scafe, S. (1985) *The Heart of the Race, Black Women's Lives in Britain*, London, Virago.

Collins, B. (1981) 'Irish Emigration to Dundee and Paisley During the First Half of the Nineteenth Century', Goldstrom, J.M., and Clarkson, L.A., (eds.), *Irish Population, Economy and Society: Essays in Honour of the late K.H. Connell*, Oxford, Oxford University Press.

Cowman, D. (1983) 'Life and Labour in Three Irish Mining Communities Circa 1840', *Saothar,* Journal of the Irish Labour History Society, Dublin, pp.10-19.

Curtis, L.P. (1971) *Apes and Angels: The Irishman in Victorian Caricature*, Newton Abbott, David and Charles.

Davidoff, L, L'Esperance, and J, Newby, H. (1976) 'Landscape with Figures: Home and Community in English Society', Mitchell, J, Oakley, A., *The Rights and Wrongs of Women*, Harmondsworth, Penguin.

Davis, G. (1991) *The Irish in Britain, 1815-1914*, Gill and Macmillan, Dublin.

Daly, M. E. 'Women in the Irish Workforce from pre-industrial to modern times, *Saothar,* Journal of the Irish Labour History Society, No.7, Dublin, 1981, p.74

Diner, H. (1983), *Erin's Daughters in America: Irish Immigrant Women in the Nineteenth Century*, Baltimore and London, The John Hopkins University Press.

Elliot, E. (1930) 'Miseries of the Poor', cited in Hammond, J.L. and B., *The Age of the Chartists 1832-1854: A Study in Discontent*, London, Longmans Green.

Engels, F. (re-published 1969) *Condition of the Working Class in England*, St. Albans, Panther Books.

Finnegan, F. (1985) 'The Irish in York', Swift, R. and Gilley, S. (eds.), *The Irish in the Victorian City*, London, Croom Helm.

Fitzpatrick, D. (1989) 'A curious middle place: the Irish in Britain, 1871-1921', Swift, R. and Gilley, S. (1989), *The Irish in Britain, 1815-1939*, London,Pinter.

Gallagher, T. (1982), *Paddy's Lament, Ireland, 1846-1847. Prelude to hatred,* Swords, Co. Dublin, Ward River Press.

Gilley, S. (1978) 'English attitudes to the Irish in England, 1780-1900', Holmes, C., (ed), *Immigrants and Minorities in British Society*, London, Allen and Unwin.

Gordon, E. (1987) 'Women, Work and Collective Action: Dundee Jute Workers 1870-1906', *Journal of Social History*, Vol.21, pp.27-47.

Gordon, E. and Breitenbach, E. (eds.) (1990) *The World is Ill Divided, Women's Work in Scotland*, Edinburgh, Edinburgh University Press.

Hakim, C. (1980) 'Census Reports as Documentary Evidence: The Census Commentaries 1801-1951', *Sociological Review*, new ser., 28, p.551-80.

Handley, J.E. (1970) *The Navvy in Scotland*, Cork, Cork University Press.

Hobsbawm, E.J. (1968) *Industry and Empire, The Pelican History of Britain*, Vol. 3, Harmondsworth, Penguin.

Horn, P. (1975) *The Rise and Fall of the Victorian Servant*, Dublin, Gill and Macmillan.

Hoult, N. (re-published 1984) 'Bridget Kiernan', Madden-Simpson, J. (ed.), *Woman's Part, an anthology of short Irish fiction by and about Irishwomen*, 1890-1960, Dublin, Arlen House.

Hunt, E.H. (1981) *British Labour History, 1815-1914*, London, Longman

Jackson, J.A. (1963) *The Irish in Britain*, London, Routledge and Kegan Paul.

Jamieson, L. (1990) 'Rural and Urban Women in Domestic Service', Gordon, E. and Breitenbach, E., (eds.), *The World is Ill Divided, Women's Work in Scotland*, Edin-. burgh, Edinburgh University Press.

John, A.V. (1984) *By the Sweat of their Brow, Women Workers at Victorian Coal Mines*, London, Routledge and Kegan Paul.

John, A.V. (ed.) (1991) *Our Mothers' Land, Chapters in Welsh Women's History, 1830-1939*, Cardiff, University of Wales Press.

Large, D. (1985) 'The Irish in Bristol in 1851', Swift, R. and Gilley, S. (eds.), *The Irish in the Victorian City*, London, Croom Helm.

Lee, J. (1973) *The Modernisation of Irish Society 1848-1918*, Dublin, Gill and Macmillan.

Lee, J. (1978) 'Women and the Church Since the Famine', MacCurtain, M and O'Corrain, D, *Women in Irish Society, The Historical Dimension*, Dublin, Arlen House.

Lees, L. H. (1979) *Exiles of Erin, Irish Migrants in Victorian London*, Manchester, Manchester University Press.

Lerner, G. (1979) *The Majority Finds Its Past, Placing Women in History*, New York and Oxford, Oxford University Press.

Lobban, R. D. (1971) 'The Irish Community in Greenock in the Nineteenth Century', *Irish Geography*, vol.vi, pp. 270-81.

MacGill, P. (1914) *Children of the dead end: the autobiography of a navvy*, London, Jenkins.

Marks, L. (1990) *Working Wives, Working Mothers: A comparative study of Irish and Jewish women's work and motherhood in East London, 1870-1914*, London, PNL Irish Studies Centre Occasional Papers Series.

Mayhew, H. (1967) *London Labour and London Poor*, Vol.1, The London Street Folk, 1851, London, Frank Cass.

McBride, T. (1976) *The Domestic Revolution, The Modernisation of Household Service in England and France, 1820-1920*, New York, Holmes and Meier.

Mokyr, J. (1983) *Why Ireland Starved: A Quantitative and Analytical History of the Irish Economy, 1800-1850*, London, George Allen and Unwin.

O'Dowd, A. (1991) *Spalpeens and Tattie Hokers, History and Folklore of the Irish Migratory Agricultural Worker in Ireland and Britain*, Blackrock, Irish Academic Press.

O'Tuathaigh, M.A.G. (1985) 'The Irish in Nineteenth-century Britain: problems of integration', Swift, R. and Gilley, S. (eds.), *The Irish in the Victorian City*, London, Croom Helm.

*Report of the State of the Irish Poor in Great Britain*, (Poor Inquiry — Ireland), London, 1835.

Rex, J. (1980) 'Immigrants and British labour: the sociological context', Lunn, K., (ed.), *Hosts, Immigrants and Minorities*, Folkestone, Dawson.

Roberts, E. (1984) *A Woman's Place: An Oral History of Working Class Women, 1890-1940*, Oxford, Basil Blackwell.

Roberts, E. (1988) *Women's Work, 1840-1940*, Studies in Economic and Social History, London, Macmillan Education,

Robertson, B.W. (1990) 'In Bondge: The Female Farm Worker in South-East Scotland', *The World is Ill Divided, Women's Work in Scotland*, Gordon, E and Breitenbach, E., Edinburgh, Edinburgh University Press.

Robinson, P. (1988) *The Women of Botany Bay*, New South Wales, Macquarie Library Press.

Ross, E. (1986) 'Labour and Love: Rediscovering London's Working-Class Mothers, 1870-1918, Lewis, J. (ed), *Labour and Love: Women's Experience of Home and Family, 1850-1940*, Oxford, Basil Blackwell.

Rowbotham, S. (1989) *The Past is Before Us: Feminism in Action Since the 1960s*, Penguin

Scott, J., Tilley, L. 'Women's Work and the Family in Nineteenth-Century Europe', *Comparative Studies in Society and History*, vol. 17, 1975, pp. 36-64

Smith, J. (1986) 'Class, skill and sectarianism in Glasgow and Liverpool, 1880-1914', R.J. Morris (ed), *Class, power and social structure in British nineteenth-century towns*, Leicester, Leicester University Press.

Treble, J. H. 'The Characteristics of the Female Unskilled Labour Market and the Formation of the Female Casual Labour Market in Glasgow, 1891-1914', *Scottish Economic and Social History*, vol. 6 (1986), pp. 33-46.

Walker, W. (1979) *Juteopolis, Dundee and its Textile Workers*, 1885-1923, Edinburgh, Scottish University Press.

Walter, B. (1989) *Gender and Irish Migration to Britain*, Geography Working Paper, 4, School of Geography, Anglia Higher Education College, Cambridge.

Williamson. J. (1986) 'The impact of the Irish on British labour markets during the industrial revolution', *Journal of Economic History*, xivi, No.3, pp. 693-721.

# 2

# Race, class and gender:
## the experience of Jewish prostitutes and other Jewish women in the East End of London at the turn of the century

*Lara Marks*

Called the world's 'oldest profession', prostitution has commonly been regarded as a permanent and unchanging trade. The study of prostitution however, illuminates many of society's social and cultural values, showing that the trade has varying functions in different societies. According to one historian, prostitution

> can function as a kind of microscopic lens through which we gain a detailed magnification of a society's organisation of class and gender; the power arrangements between men and women; women's economic and social status; the prevailing sexual ideology; the underlying class relations that govern different groups' access to political and economic resources; the ways in which female erotic and procreative sexuality are channelled into specific institutional arrangements; and the cross-class alliances and antagonisms between reformers and prostitutes.[1]

All too often, in examining the social and economic conditions giving rise to prostitution, it is easy to overlook the effect that it had on the lives of individuals, particularly those of women. Women have not only been victims of the trade but also active participants. Racism reveals an extra dimension to the study of prostitution, which this chapter explores in the context of the Jewish community. Many of the insecurities of gender, class and sexuality were reinforced by the position of Jewish women. They were not only vulnerable as working-class women in the Jewish community and in the outside world but they also faced the difficulties of anti-semitism. In order to understand how the forces of sexuality, class and gender affected the experience of Jewish women, it is necessary to examine the structures of the Jewish and outside communities and how these acted against women and drove many into prostitution.

The economic and social dislocation in Eastern Europe and the resulting Jewish migration in the late nineteenth century coincided with a time when prostitution was becoming established in a world-wide network, making Jewish immigrants particularly susceptible to the trade. Moreover, Jewish immigrants in the East End of London came into an area where prostitution was already widespread and could not be avoided.

This chapter focuses on the ways in which Jewish women became involved in the trade and considers how their experiences were different from non-Jewish prostitutes. It also explores the role class and gender played in the response of established Jewish leaders to the white slave traffic and the attitude of wider society to Jewish involvement in prostitution.

Initially stimulated by the passing of the Contagious Diseases (CD) Acts in 1864, 1866 and 1869, prostitution, and in particular 'social purity' were hotly debated issues in Britain during the latter half of the nineteenth century. Although the CD Acts were primarily concerned with the spread of venereal diseases amongst the armed forces, calling for stringent medical investigations of prostitutes, they focused on the women, not the men involved. This created what was seen as the double standard whereby men were able to satisfy their sexual desires without responsibility, while women paid the penalty.

The 1860s signalled the beginning of a long campaign to challenge the ideology promoted by the CD Acts. Many women repealers, such as Josephine Butler, cried out against the discriminatory double standard and the degrading conditions which prostitutes faced. With the withdrawal of the CD Acts in the 1880s, attention increasingly turned to the white slave trade. Many deplored the idea that innocent women, often lured initially by the promise of marriage, could be shipped off to a foreign land where they would be abused and pushed into prostitution.

Prior to the passage of the CD Acts, prostitution was not an established or regular trade. Women moved in and out of prostitution depending on what other employment was available. Many chose to become prostitutes instead of working in degrading, poorly paid, and arduous trades, or turned to prostitution during slack seasons when other work was scarce and economic survival impossible. In these circumstances prostitution was mainly a trade run by women, and they were able to determine when and where they worked. With the repeal of the CD Acts in the 1880s, prostitution became more regulated. This involved growing restrictions and harassment by the police, and ultimately forced many prostitutes off the streets. Prostitutes were no longer free agents, able to bargain for their own clients. Instead they were pushed to rely on third party agents, who were often as brutal as the police. Madams and prostitutes were now controlled by pimps and crime syndicates and were no longer their own bosses. Prostitution thus became a complex system and was no longer merely a profession run by women.[2]

The growth in British colonies and in the Empire created another avenue for the prostitution trade. The chronic shortage of women in recently established colonial settlements, such as the gold mines on the Witwatersrand in South Africa, generated a 'need' for white women, which the white slave trade partly fulfilled.[3] This was a highly structured international network, dependent on Europe for recruits, some of whom were drawn from the Jewish ghettos of Eastern Europe.

It was no coincidence that Jewish participation in the trade increased at a time when the Jewish community in Eastern Europe was being torn apart and scattered all over the world. Some had travelled from towns, others from little villages. Their migration was part of a general movement west from Eastern Europe and was caused partly by the congestion of the Jewish population in this area. During the nineteenth century the Jewish birth rate was double that of the Russian one, which in itself was very high. Between 1800-1897 the Jewish population in the Russian empire had multiplied from 1,000,000 to over 5,189,000. Although these figures underestimate the true population size in the Russian empire, because they fail to take into account the large number of Jews who had already emigrated, they demonstrate an enormous increase in the Jewish population. Such growth had also occurred in other parts of Eastern Europe.[4]

Life for the Jewish community in the Russian Empire was much like the life Jews had in other parts of Eastern Europe. Tzarist policies had imposed enormous restrictions on the Jewish population in Russia and other areas, not only in geographical location, but also in employment capability and mobility. The May laws of 1881 forced most Jews out of rural villages into the (more urbanised) towns and cities of the Pale of Settlement (North West Russia) and this was intensified by the prohibition on Jews to acquire rural property after 1882. Within the Pale of Settlement, Jewish workers tended to be employed in very small artisanal workshops and had scant opportunity for work in large factories, especially as these were located largely outside the settlement, where only a few Jews could go. In addition, Jewish workers often lacked the latest technical skills and anti-semitism further restricted their employment possibilities, so did religious observance: factory owners were reluctant to employ Jews because they would not work on Saturdays.

This left the Jews no alternative but to pursue artisanal occupations, mostly in the garment industry. Such work often entailed a menial existence, because Jewish artisans working in small workshops could no longer compete with the factories. Jews who had previously been skilled artisans were now displaced by machines. This was an important cause of much of their poverty, and was intensified by the competition for employment within the Jewish community. By 1900, 30-35% of the Jewish population of Russia and Poland were receiving aid from Jewish welfare and charitable institutions.[5]

Pogroms and persecution further aggravated the situation. Although Jews had begun to emigrate in large numbers in the 1870s, this process escalated in the following decades. The assassination of Tzar Alexander II in 1881 led to anti-Jewish riots in Kherson, Kiev and Odessa, which spread to other parts of the Russian empire. Although small in scale, further anti-semitic enactments and pogroms in Russia in the 1890s were sufficient to maintain anxiety. All these events increased the urge to migrate west.

Between 1881 and 1905 about a million Jews left Eastern Europe, three-quarters of them came from Russia. Over 80% went to America, others migrated to Western Europe, South America and South Africa. Those who came to England were mostly from Russian Poland, but some Galicians and Rumanians also arrived in the period 1890-1902. Between 1881 and 1914, about 100,000-150,000 Jews came to Britain. The Census of 1901 showed 95,425 Russians and Poles living in the United Kingdom, of whom 53,537 had settled in the County of London.[6]

Social and economic dislocation in East Europe together with migration often disrupted traditional Jewish communal life. For the most part, the family unit remained essential to the social fabric of the Jewish community, providing security in an alien world, but the conventional marriage traditions altered with migration. The migration of large numbers of young men meant that many eligible women who were conventionally expected to marry were left behind with no prospect of finding a partner. As one East European emigrant, Mary Antin, wrote, the lack of education and the weight of tradition, made spinsterhood 'the greatest misfortune that could threaten a girl, and to ward off that calamity the girl and her family ... would strain every nerve.'[7]

Not surprisingly the chance to marry and emigrate abroad was attractive. A Jewish agency that was combating Jewish involvement in the white slave trade argued that:

> In Russia, Rumania and Galicia the conditions under which the Jews are largely forced to live is a direct incentive to the White Slave traffic. Girls are only too glad to escape from the weariness and grinding poverty of homes where they are often not allowed to learn a trade. Their parents, seeing seemingly eligible young men come to their villages, eagerly give their daughters to them in marriage or entrust them to their care in order to have 'excellent situations' found for them abroad.[8]

The Jewish marriage contract created specific difficulties for Jewish women, making the procurer's task that much simpler. A couple could be married with only one witness and did not require a formal ceremony. It was therefore easy for a procurer to 'marry' and take his newly wedded wife to a foreign land, where he could then sell her into a brothel. As one American woman reformer admitted, 'the acute horror among the Jews of the state of being an old maid makes the swindling of Jewish women under the promise of marriage especially easy.' The dire poverty faced by East European Jewish communities also made the selling of Jewish women an economic necessity for some.

> Whoever knows the hair-raising poverty and subjection of the Jews there, will understand that it can happen that a father could sell his daughter in order to provide the most necessary means of sustenance for his other children.[9]

Migration also disrupted the marriage patterns of those who were already married, when wives and husbands were separated, which could sometimes lead to estrangement or desertion. According to Jewish law, women were the property of their husbands. They could not initiate a divorce but had to depend on their husbands granting them permission to divorce, giving them a *get*. Without a *get*, or proof of widowhood, women could not remarry. With the wars and pogroms wrenching the Jewish community apart in Eastern Europe, it was not uncommon for Jewish women to find themselves in this position. At a congress held during the First World War, it was estimated that 25,000 women in Poland were facing *agunah* (widowhood) because their husbands disappeared during the war. And many women found themselves deserted by husbands who left no trace of their new address. Without a husband and without the right to remarry, the Jewish woman frequently had no support.

Whilst conditions in Eastern Europe led to greater insecurities for Jewish women, their tenuous position was reinforced when they settled in East London and became subject to the structure and attitudes of Anglo-Jews and wider English society. The Jewish population was made up of different social classes: those who had been established in Britain for a long time and the newcomers. The earliest Jews to arrive, in the mid-seventeenth century, were of Sephardi (Spanish and Portuguese) descent, but from the late seventeenth century onwards, Jewish immigrants tended to be Ashkenazi (German and Eastern European) in origin. The groups differed in how they pronounced Hebrew, their cultural traditions, language, and also in their organisation of charitable relief. Such differences could cause conflict — often class conflict. By the mid-nineteenth century established Anglo-Jews had achieved some financial security, but their political position was still tenuous. They won some civil rights in the 1850s but were still unsure about their status within British society. This uncertainty dominated their relationship with the Jewish newcomers from Eastern Europe and it accentuated social stratifications amongst the Jews. Many of the more established found the poverty and traditions of the new East European immigrants strange and embarrassing and this was often reflected in the charitable organisations they established for the newcomers.

Many of the more elite Anglo-Jews were most concerned about anti-semitism. While anti-semitism in England had not, since the Middle Ages, assumed the violent character which it often took in other parts of Europe, it was nonetheless prevalent in late nineteenth century Britain. A liberal political culture and a tradition of offering asylum were well entrenched, but while Catholics obtained civil liberties in 1829, Jews were not granted the same rights until 1858. In literature and journalism the Jew was frequently stereotyped as a mean and rich financier with the ambition and capacity to dominate the world. Interestingly, the Jew was also portrayed as weak and sickly and a carrier of disease, a caricature often applied to the East European immigrants, whose physique was indeed often puny. This characteristic of maintaining two totally contra-dictory stereotypes simultaneously is characteristic of anti-semitism. Hostility towards the Jews was still widespread at the turn of the century. A letter written by G. Bingham Ward to the *East London Observer*, during the agitation for a restriction on alien immigration in 1905, typified the contradictory stereotyping:

> Sir — There is not the slightest doubt that the principal cause of distress amongst the working-class is the competition of these foreign Jews, who are filling our big towns ... The first thing these people do on arriving is to turn round and see the best way they can take the bread out the mouths of the natives of the country that shelters them. How much longer will the British working man stand this kind of thing. We don't massacre the Jews here, we simply allow them to swarm here and starve us out. Meanwhile the rich Jews (notably a certain millionaire) are coining money by buying streets of houses, putting up models in their place, which they let at exorbitant rent to their compatriots (25 November 1905).

A great proportion of the Jews who had emigrated from Eastern Europe in the 1880s came to live in the East End of London. In 1905 Jews comprised approximately forty per cent of the inhabitants in Stepney; out of a population of 298,610, 119,800 were Jews. The figures are hard to calculate accurately because census data categorised Jews along with non-Jewish Russian immigrants. Settling in the East End, the Jewish immigrants became visible in a wider focus on the plight of the area.

During the nineteenth century, social observers had been increasingly concentrating on the evils of the East End and the pollution that spread from it to the more respectable areas of London. The East End was seen as a den for all the social vices of theft, prostitution and alcoholism. It was a district of great poverty, overcrowding and slums. For many who lived there, life was a struggle to earn even a few pennies to buy their daily bread. Employment was difficult to find, especially on a permanent basis in the unskilled market. Most of the population were working-class and employed as casual labourers. There was already much hardship and competition, and the arrival of more people only worsened these social conflicts and the fight for resources.

The British Brothers' League, an organisation specifically established to campaign for legislative restrictions on immigration, together with many other sub-groups, manipulated social issues within local areas which were causing grievance and channelled them into hostility towards Jewish immigrants. Anti-semitism offered a useful tool for eliminating any sympathy caused by social deprivation and a convenient explanation for the underlying causes of people's poverty. Such bitterness is evident from how close the area came to a pogrom over the Jack the Ripper affair in 1888.[10] Much of the anti-semitism in the East End of London was fostered by the already appalling conditions under which the population was living. Jews were seen, like their Irish predecessors, as the perpetrators rather than the victims, of overcrowding, shortage of housing and unemployment. Jewish immigrants were also accused of immorality and dirty habits.

The Royal Commission on Alien Immigration in 1903 reflected similar opinions, among the members of Parliament themselves. Liberals, however, argued that the Jews should, according to the doctrines of *laissez-faire*, be allowed free entry into Britain, whereas the Conservatives, in office between 1895 and 1905, advocated some kind of protection against the influx of immigrants. Between 1892 and 1906 anti-alien issues played a key role in the election campaigns of many Conservative candidates, and in the 1905 Aliens Act.

Sexual hostility and debates about morality frequently featured in the anti-alien agitation. Arnold White, a leading figure in this campaign, stigmatised the Jew as a member of a physically and mentally inferior race, 'a keeper of gambling halls and disorderly houses, a procurer and a bully ... Procuring for the 'white slave' trade, and living upon the earnings of women, are now two of the regular professions of the alien Jew.'[11] Such writings only enhanced the feelings of unease amongst the Jewish communal leaders, who saw Jewish involvement in prostitution as a source of deep embarrassment, a slur on their own respectability. Although the numbers were never accurately measured, even a tiny number of Jews involved in prostitution constituted a real danger for the Jewish community. As the German-Jewish feminist Bertha Pappenheim expressed it: 'If we admit the existence of the traffic our enemies decry us, if we deny it, they say we are trying to conceal it.' It is estimated that approximately a thousand Jews were employed in the trade in Britain.[12] The proportion of Jews arrested for prostitution was higher than for any other group. Data collected from before the First World War shows that 20 per cent of the convictions for brothel-keeping were against Jews in the East End Borough of Stepney.[13] Admittedly, such figures might reflect a bias against Jews, rather than an accurate gauge of the numbers of Jews involved in the trade.

While precise figures of Jewish involvement are unavailable, the extent of the concern it caused amongst the Jewish community was important. Not only could prostitution lead to anti-semitism, but it also challenged the Jewish ethics on sex and the status of women. Fears of anti-semitism, as well as the concern for the plight of Jewish women, spurred action within the Jewish community. In a short time the Jewish philanthropic organisations were at the forefront of the activities opposing the white slave traffic. One of the most important agencies involved in this work was the Jewish Association for the Protection of Girls and Women (JAPGW), set up in 1885. Based in London, the JAPGW became the headquarters for world-wide networks. Rescue homes and ladies' visitors programmes were set up to try and befriend young girls and protect their innocence, and 'Gentlemen's Committees' established to send representatives to meet the incoming unaccompanied women at the ports. Special shelters were established to greet unaccompanied young Jewish women. Non-Jewish women were also helped by these organisations. For those who had 'fallen' irredeemably, there was the Charcroft Home for unmarried mothers, which provided accommodation for a year and possibilities of employment in domestic service. Adoption was arranged for their babies.[14]

The majority of East European Jewish immigrants arrived with no money and from a working-class background, all of which caused much embarrassment to middle-class Anglo-Jews. Communication between the two groups was difficult, because unlike the new immigrants, the established community did not speak Yiddish. Overcrowding and the breakdown of the social unit, the nuclear family, were also frequently blamed on the immigrants, creating further insecurity amongst Jewish communal leaders. For the settled Jews the influx of newcomers threatened their newly-won status and respectability. They not only feared anti-semitism but were also genuinely concerned about the finite resources available for their poorer brethren through the auspices of the

Jewish Board of Guardians. For these reasons, some Anglo-Jews tried their utmost to discourage new Jewish immigrants from remaining in Britain and to help them on to America and South Africa. In some instances Jewish communal leaders even supported the idea of repatriation and certain of the restrictions advocated by the Aliens Bill.[15]

Newcomers who remained in Britain faced a rigorous programme of anglicisation. A leader comment in the community's newspaper, *The Jewish Chronicle*, in 1881 observed:

> We may not be able to make them rich, but we may hope to render them English in feeling and in conduct ... By improving in all directions and educating their children in an English fashion, we can do much to change our brethren poor into brethren who shall not only be Jews, but English Jews.[16]

Such attitudes often reinforced the class divisions amongst the Jews. Anglicisation was not simply the enforcement of more middle-class values on the newcomers by the more established Jews but a complex process dependent on the cultural and social circumstances of the newcomers as well as their aspirations. This had important implications for men and women's gender roles in the home and the workplace.

At times anglicisation could result in a strengthening of gender stereotypes. In Louis Golding's novel *Magnolia Street*, written in 1910, an Anglo-Jewish character, Mr Emmanuel, observes when watching the Jewish children playing in the street that:

> In these few years of their boyhood and girlhood, they had become more impregnated with English than other foreigners might in two generations. He saw the small boys conforming to the type of small boys opposite. They played football and cricket, and studied the team score with, if anything, more passion. They became, or yearned to be 'sports', and 'decent chaps'. Just as successfully, the little girls were becoming English 'misses'.[17]

Although it is debatable how far these gender stereotypes held, the middle-class image of the male breadwinner and the female homemaker was an important influence on the nature and structure of the support given by Anglo-Jewish charitable organisations. Emphasis on the domestic role of women was apparent throughout the Jewish and non-Jewish philanthropic institutions set up to rescue prostitutes and unmarried mothers. Most of these organisations claimed that the women they were helping were innocent and in need of protection and correct schooling in duties of being a wife and a mother. Accordingly, girls in Charcroft House, the Jewish home for unmarried mothers, were taught not only to read and write, but also the art of cookery, laundry and household work, which, it was reported, had a positive influence in making their manners softer, their speech less surly, and 'their habits more domestic'.[18]

Such work was compatible with the more traditional image and role of women in Judaism, which pictured women as the domestic homemaker and mother, seeing to the needs of her family. These images, however, changed in intensity over time. In Eastern Europe, a Jewish woman's worth was measured in particular by her ability to support her husband financially and domestically while he pursued his religious studies. Many Jewish men aimed to marry into a more middle-class family which could afford to keep both him and his wife while he studied, but less middle-class women had to support the family if the man was to study. For these women work was not a stigma, but a religious good deed. Isaac Singer's description of his grandmother stresses this:

> She was a saintly woman who never assumed that it was her husband's duty to support her. She left him to his beloved Torah and [Kabala] and herself travelled to Warsaw to buy goods and earn a living for her family, since her husband's wages [as a rabbi] could not keep a bird alive ... It never occurred to her that one day her precious son would be expected to earn a living. She always considered this a wife's responsibility.[19]

In this environment, ideally, men were raised to enter the world of scholastic education, and not the world of business, leaving financial matters to their wives. Often this pattern was repeated in England, as one woman remembered:

> My father possessed a basic inadequacy which, to the present day, I am unable to understand. He seemed quite unable to cope with the day to day struggle of making a living, and apart from one or two brief periods, could neither provide for himself nor for his family ... He tried business and was not so much no good at it, as he was fundamentally uninterested in making money. Unlike mother, he was a poor judge of people and believed only good of everybody. Neither could he bear to be shut away in a factory'.[20]

In families in which men did not pursue religious study, women's involvement in the family income was still necessary. As poorly paid artisans, Jewish men could not earn enough to support a family. For these women no distinction was drawn between home and the workplace. It was merely seen as another part of managing the home. Jewish women found a wide range of means to earn a living: running shops, peddling, selling on market stalls, sewing clothes, washing, baking. In some rural areas women worked in gardens picking fruit and gathering berries.[21]

Although by Western standards many of these women's work patterns could be considered masculine, they were similar to those found in other pre-industrial societies where men and women shared with their husbands the burden of supporting the family in addition to their other responsibilities. What distinguished Jewish women, however, was that they were sometimes the sole support of their families, whilst their husbands devoted themselves to religious study.[22]

This situation prevailed until the last quarter of the nineteenth century. Thereafter the social and economic dislocation, as well as ideas from the West, began to modify certain Jewish values in Eastern Europe. The prestige of male scholarship began to diminish and women's working patterns altered. These changes were reinforced with the impact of emigration. Increasingly, a family's social status was marked by the ability of a husband to maintain his wife in the 'leisurely' role of wife and mother. In accordance with this image women were not expected to work. As one Jewish woman born in Manchester in 1902 to immigrant parents stated,

> In those days, not the rule but the custom was — a girl got married — a Jewish girl got married — it was her duty to stay at home and look after her home and husband and have his meal ready, and a nice, clean home and fire to come home to ... Those days, a man was king of his castle.[23]

Although it is questionable how quickly this change occurred, evidence suggests that in the space of within one generation Jewish women began to remain more in the home. Testimonies during the Royal Commission on Alien Immigration in 1903 indicated that Jewish women were far less likely to be working outside the home than the women of the host population in the East End, which many witnesses claimed was the explanation for the good health of Jewish infants and children.[24] Given the high proportion of Jews who were working at home in sweated industries, such remarks on the good health of Jewish mothers and their infants are surprising, perhaps explained by the fact that Jewish mothers could combine the tasks of motherhood more easily with such home piecework than work pursued outside the home. The rapidity with which the Jewish immigrants were able to prosper economically also might explain why women increasingly were able to remain in the home. Many of these immigrants were probably less observant and concerned with the prestige of male scholarship than those who remained in Eastern Europe, and so found the notion of the male breadwinner much more acceptable. Religious families who did migrate found that they often had to compromise their religious observance in England if they were to survive economically.

Not all Jewish women, however, could afford to remain at the home but had to contribute to the family income. Men's wages were often a pittance. Support systems were eroded with the onset of massive emigration and scattering of communities and many women found themselves separated from their husbands. So women increasingly found they had to support themselves. They had to look for alternative forms of income to marriage, and could not afford to take on the role of the leisurely lady. Even married women were forced to supplement their husbands' income by undertaking piece-work within the home. Some took in lodgers to help pay the rent and feed the family. Others ran shops or became tallies. Those considered less fortunate undertook cleaning and washing for others.[25]

Many women worked in sweated industries based in the home — mainly needlework. The more fortunate and skilled women earned 2d. an hour but most had to content themselves with ¾d.[26] One woman remembered the appalling conditions that her mother toiled under:

> It was Mother's job to sew the hooks and eyes in very securely because of the weight of the jackets. There was a piece-work system and Mother was paid a penny farthing for such a heavy form of tailoring, Mother's hands became very swollen and she earned next to nothing.[27]

Those less fortunate frequently joined the ranks of unemployed women in East London, where work was especially hard to procure. This was even more difficult for Jewish women, who often had to face the handicap of anti-semitism in the labour market. The absence of state provision for unemployment meant that many unemployed women were forced to depend on charity. Such aid, however, was not easily obtained and was continually associated with pauperisation. Jewish women had the additional problem that in the outside world, they were frequently ineligible for non-Jewish charity support. Immigrants in the workhouse also faced a very tenuous position, worsened by the Aliens Act. According to the Act, the Home Secretary was empowered to deport aliens who had been proven by a court to have been, within 12 months of arrival, 'in receipt of any such parochial relief' in a workhouse or had been 'found wandering without ostensible means of subsistence'.[28]

Faced with discrimination in the outside community, Jewish women often found scant support within it, as was true for deserted wives. Frequently a Jewish woman would arrive from Eastern Europe, following her husband, only to discover that he was not there, or that they were no longer compatible, or that he was with another woman. According to Jewish law, if she did not have her husband's permission to divorce or *get*, or proof that her husband was dead, a deserted Jewish wife was unable to remarry and provide for herself in that way.

The plight of deserted wives was made worse by Jewish law for deserted wives, which made no allowance for the situation and thus hindered their ability to secure financial support. The Jewish Board of Guardians would sometimes spend a great deal of money trying to find the husbands, rather than provide economic support for the woman and her children. A statement made in 1902 epitomised the approach taken by the Board of Guardians:

> To compel these women to enter the workhouse is at the same time the best test of their deserted and destitute condition, the greatest deterrent to this course of conduct on the part of men, and the most practical way of compelling them to resume their proper responsibility for the support of their families.[29]

Exclusion from both the host society and the Jewish charitable institutions would leave women with little alternative but to turn to prostitution to support themselves. Whichever way the Jewish woman turned she met with discrimination. Lacking charitable support and faced with a menial existence in the labour market, prostitution could seem an attractive alternative, as portrayed by one writer:

> Rosie had worked for years in sweatshops, saving money to bring her parents from Europe. Then she fell sick. Her savings melted. She went to hospital. She came out, and could not find a job. She was hungry, feeble and alone. No one cared whether she lived or died.

She was ready for the river. A pimp met her. He took her to a restaurant and fed her her first solid meal. He made her a practical offer. Rosie accepted. She never regretted her choice: it was far easier than being in a sweatshop.[30]

In 1910, one Jewish prostitute found that she could earn between £1 and £2 with each client. Sometimes she was able to amass as much as £15, a sum which surpassed any she could gain through other work. But prostitution had its hazards. This prostitute was forced, under physical threats, to hand over at least half or more of her earnings to her 'pimp'.[31] Of two other alien Jewish women who were convicted for soliciting and disorderly conduct in East London, one was given a sentence of six weeks hard labour, and the other fined 40s. In addition the judge ordered that they both be deported.[32]

Once in prostitution, some women preferred to remain in the profession than to return to their previous life-style, as illustrated by the case of Fanny Epstein. Born in Warsaw, Fanny came to London with her parents, where she gained work as a 'fur machine hand' for only a short period and was then unemployed. At the age of eighteen she was restless at home with her parents and impatient with a long marriage engagement. She soon became attracted by the friendship of Alexander Kahn.

He was thirty-four, well-dressed, seemingly prosperous. He would have liked to marry her, he said, but his divorce had not yet come through. By what must have seemed a happy coincidence, he had a friend, Isaac Stirling, who knew a friend of Fanny's, Annie Gould. They planned an adventure together. Fanny secretly left her home in Whitechapel and met her friends at Cannon Street Station. There they took the boat train for Paris, where they stayed for a week.

Her father, a tailor, searched for Fanny in Paris but to no avail. He appealed to the National Vigilance Association, which worked together with the police to rescue women trapped by the white slave procurers. Eventually she was discovered to have been taken by white slave agents to Bombay, where she was running a saloon bar/brothel. Once found she declined the help of the police and declared that she was working of her own free will. She refused to return home, finding Bombay and her occupation much more exciting than her previous existence with her parents in East London, and providing the independence she wanted.[33]

The average age of Jewish prostitutes ranged from fifteen to twenty-five years, which suggests that for many prostitution was a transient profession. However, it could stigmatise a woman for life. Chastity was a highly prized virtue, not only in non-Jewish middle-class circles but also in the Jewish community. Jewish rituals concerning sex and cleanliness fuelled the notion that Jewish prostitutes were 'unclean' and 'impure', and often resulted in ostracism. Although more established middle-class Jews bitterly criticised prostitution, recent immigrants familiar with destitution and poverty were more sympathetic, regarding prostitution as a 'natural' way of life.[34]

Prostitutes did not necessarily see themselves as unclean and ineligible for participating in religious life. Jewish prostitutes often retained their religious identity, indeed some pimps and prostitutes set up their own mutual sickness clubs and burial assistance schemes, as well as established communal institutions, including synagogues and burial grounds. In the 1890s in Buenos Aires arrangements were made by a pimp for Jewish prostitutes to attend a synagogue just for the high holidays. By 1913 they had a permanent synagogue.

> Given the hardships, loneliness, and contempt that women endured, it is not surprising that some sought to maintain religious customs, especially in remote places. Up in Butte, Montana, Jewish prostitutes were said never to work on religious holidays ... In London Jews were said to shy away from Christian rescue homes from fear of eating non-kosher food, or even fear of conversion.[35]

The Jewish prostitute symbolised the tenuous position and vulnerability of Jewish women in general. Jewish middle-class women involved in the campaign to combat the white slave trade, while concerned with the oppression facing Jewish women, evidenced certain contradictions in their aims. Although they attacked the economic causes underlying prostitution and the specific Jewish marriage laws and customs, they never made religious ruling a central part of their platform. While they condemned the problems of obtaining a *get* and the plight of deserted wives, they did not call for the total abolition of Jewish laws concerning marriage, and instead urged rabbis to allow couples civil as well as religious weddings, as security for the woman's position in the future.

The campaigns of the Jewish women reformers, their goals and their successes, demonstrate their own susceptibilities in the Jewish communities and the outside world. As in the case of non-Jewish women, Jewish women were reliant on men for economic and political power to achieve their reforms, and because the white slave trade was organised internationally, women were greatly dependent on government reforms. The most they could hope to achieve was to offer women protection and rescue them from the potential hazards of prostitution. Their action, therefore, tended to focus on the establishment of rescue homes and lady visitors rather than on more encompassing social and economic reforms.

Men were designated the more 'dangerous' tasks of meeting unaccompanied women at the ports, where there was the possibility of confrontations with procurers. A debate within the JAPGW on women's participation in the cases' committee, work mostly allocated to men, reveals the fears that were expressed about women's involvement in curbing prostitution. In 1919 women were allowed to sit on the Cases Committee, but not without some reservations, because as it was stated, 'So many of the ladies did not consider the danger of libel and the limitations of the law, etc, and they would require to learn a great deal.' By 1919, however, it was thought that times had changed and 'now even young women spoke of matters without any privacy' whereas in the past they would not have dared to touch certain cases handled by the Gentlemen's Committee.[36] A man was always present to consult on the Jewish women's committees, but women mostly performed the routine work.

Nevertheless, as in the case of non-Jewish women, the action taken by Jewish women in combating white slavery was productive in that it raised their consciousness and pushed women into the political arena for the first time.

> It was far more effective to attempt to elevate the legal, social, and economic status of women as well as their self-images by using arguments based upon saving the Jewish community from the scourge of prostitution rather than demanding equality for women. Thus the white slavery issue was a sincere one which also served wider feminist goals.[37]

By participating in philanthropic work, middle-class Jewish women were breaking down the stereotypes of their own status. Many of the barriers to women's participation in philanthropy had diminished by 1902, as witnessed by the first International Jewish Women's Conference held in London that year.[38] By moving into philanthropy, women stepped out of the private sphere of the home and began to move into the public arena. In a world that was divided between public and private, this was of considerable importance.

Whatever the increased political awareness caused by the philanthropic activities of these women reformers, the conflict between middle-class and working-class expectations was never fully resolved. Philanthropy could patch up the problems caused by poverty, but it could not eliminate their underlying causes. It was also difficult for middle-class reformers to understand fully why women took up prostitution and were willing to sell their own bodies, when middle-class women were so ardently fighting against the abuse of their bodies and their right to determine access to them.

## Conclusion

Jewish prostitution and involvement in the white slave trade cannot be seen simply as a traffic of innocent young women, as it has commonly been portrayed by contemporaries and subsequent Jewish historians. It was the result of a more complex combination of social and economic forces as well as the particular vulnerabilities created by Jewish customs and traditions. To some extent the reports of the JAPGW portray some understanding of the causes of Jewish prostitution:

> Girls disappear and cannot be traced, others by serious offers of lucrative employment by promises of marriage, indeed even by marriage itself, are taken from their homes, and then with heartless cunning are led step by step ... They are gradually lured on until they come to forfeit all sense of modesty, and to lose their love for all that is pure and noble. Girls whose lives are spent in the grinding struggle of constant toil to earn four or five shillings a week, are tempted away by description of the delights of an easy luxurious life. Too late they discover the pain, violence and slavery by which they have to submit, and the mental misery which the sinful life entails.[39]

Yet, if the case of Fanny Epstein is to be understood, not all these women who participated in the trade felt they were victims, and some indeed did not wish to be redeemed. Often women chose prostitution as a means of evading more degrading positions afforded them. Had Victorian reformers pushing for change in prostitution seen prostitutes as live social agents, they may have been forced to see that the causes of prostitution lay in the exploitative structure of society and the poverty that prevailed amongst women, which demanded much more extensive social and economic reforms.

This study has shown how race, class and gender operated in a complexity of ways both in shaping Jewish women's participation in prostitution and in their fight against it. For all the women involved, anti-semitism was a powerful discriminating force which prompted migration from Russia and influenced the reception they had in British society and from Anglo-Jews. Keen to promote their respectability, Anglo-Jews saw wives and mothers as key figures in promoting to the outside world the strong Jewish traditions of family life and morality. Jewish involvement in prostitution therefore not only constituted a threat to this image and added fuel to anti-semitic protagonists but it also exposed the vulnerability of Jewish women as a result of the upheaval caused by migration and the restrictions imposed on women by Jewish marriage laws.

## Notes

1.  R. Rosen (1992) *The Lost Sisterhood: Prostitution in America 1900-1918* (John Hopkins University Press, Baltimore, 1982).
2.  J. Walkowitz, *Prostitution and Victorian Society* (Cambridge University Press, Cambridge, 1981).
3.  See C. Van Onselen, *Studies in the Social and Economic History of the Witwater- srand 1886-1913 Vol I — New Babylon* (Longman, Johannesburg, London, 1982).
4.  L. P. Gartner, *The Jewish Immigration in England* (Columbia University, London, 1960), 21.
5.  Gartner, *The Jewish Immigration in England*, 21; Z. Y. Gitelman, *Jewish Nationality and Soviet Policies* (Princeton, 1972), 19.
6.  V. D. Lipman, *Social History of the Jews 1850-1950* (Watts, London, 1954), 89-90.
7.  M. Antin, *The Promised Land* (Princeton, 1911, 1985), 35.
8.  Jewish Association for the Protection of Girls and Women (JAPGW) *Annual Report* (hereafter A/R) (1908), p.19.
9.  M. Kaplan, *The Jewish Feminist Movement in Germany 1904-1938* (Greenwood Press, Westport., Conn., London, 1979), 110, 116.
10. C. Bermant, *Point of Arrival* (Eyre Methuen, London, 1975), 112, and J. R. Walko- witz, 'Jack the Ripper and the Myth of Male Violence', *Feminist Studies*, Vol. 8, No.3 (1982), 543-75.
11. *The Standard*, 30 Jan. 1911.
12. E. J. Bristow, *Vice and Vigilance* (Gill and Macmillan, Dublin), 180; L. P. Gartner, 'Anglo-Jewry and the Jewish International Traffic in Prostitution', *Association of Jewish Studies Review*. vol. 7-8, (1982-1983), 129-78, p.160.
13. E. J. Bristow, *Prostitution and Prejudice* (Clarendon, Oxford, 1982), 237.
14. JAPGW *A/Rs* (1887-1940). See also L. Marks, '"The Luckless Waifs and Strays of Humanity": Irish and Jewish Immigrant Unwed Mothers in London, 1870-1939', *Twentieth Century British History*, Vol. 3, No.2 (1992), 113-37.
15. D. M. Feldman, 'Immigrants and Workers, Englishmen and Jews: Jewish Immigra- tion to the East End of London', Ph.D. thesis, (Cambridge University, 1985), 203-5,

and 277; S. Cohen, 'Anti-Semitism, Immigration Controls and the Welfare State', *Critical Social Policy,* Issue 13 (1985), 77-8.

16. *Jewish Chronicle*, 12 Aug. 1881.
17. L. Golding, *Magnolia Street* (London, 1932), 191-2.
18. JAPGW, *A/R* (1897-98).
19. Cited in Baum et. al. *The Jewish Woman*, 68.
20. B. Aronovitch, *Give It Time* (London, 1974), 14, 19.
21. Baum, et al., *The Jewish Woman* and S. Glenn, *Daughters of the Shtetl* (Cornell University Press, Ithaca, 1990), chapter 1.
22. Baum et al., *The Jewish Woman*, 67, 68; J. Scott, and L. A. Tilly, 'Women's Work and the Family in 19th Century Europe' in C. E. Rosenberg, (ed.), *The Family in History* (University of Pennsylvannia Press, Philadelphia, 1975).
23. Interview B1 in R. Burman, 'The Jewish Woman as Breadwinner', *Oral History*, Vol. 10, No.2 (1982), 27-39, p.27.
24. J. Prag, *Royal Commission on Alien Immigration*, Parliamentary Papers 1903 IX, Q17877. For more discussion on Jewish infants' health see L. Marks, *Model Mothers: Jewish Mothers and Maternity Provision in East London, 1870-1939* (Oxford University Press, Oxford, 1994).
25. L. Marks, 'Working Wives and Working Mothers: A Comparative Study of Irish and East European Jewish Married Women's Work and Motherhood in East London 1870-1914', Polytechnic of North London, Irish Studies Centre, *Occasional Papers Series*, No.2 (London 1990).
26. C. Booth, *Life and Labour of the People in London* 17 vols (A.M. Kelly, London, 1901-03, 1969), *Industry,* IV, 63.
27. Aronovitch, *Give It Time*, 18.
28. *Jewish Chronicle*, 24 June 1910.
29. *Jewish Chronicle*, 30 May 1902.
30. M. Gold, *Jews Without Money* (New York, 1930, 1958), 34.
31. *East London Observer*, 21 May 1910, p.2.
32. *East London Observer*, 17 Feb. 1906, p.3.
33. K. Ballhatchet, *Race, Sex and Class under the Raj: Imperial Attitudes and Policies and their Critics,* (Weidenfeld and Nicholson, London, 1980), 126-9.
34. J. White, *Rothschild Buildings: Life in an East End Tenement Block, 1887-1920* (Routledge, London, 1980), 124-5.
35. Bristow, *Prostitution and Prejudice*, 123, 140-1.
36. JAPGW, Gentleman's Committee, Minutes, 14 May 1919.
37. Kaplan, *The Jewish Feminist Movement,* p.137; J. R. Walkowitz, 'The Politics of Prostitution' *History Workshop Journal*, Issue 13 (1982), 80-9.
38. See R. Burman's chapter in this volume.
39. JAPGW *A/R* (1897-1898), pp.21-2.

# 3

# William Brown and other Women: Black women in London c1740-1840

*Joan Grant*

This chapter offers an overview of the lives of black women in Britain over the century c1740-1838, when black women came to Britain from many places, mostly West Africa and the Caribbean but also other European countries and South America. They faced a double oppression based upon race and gender. Pro-slavery writers evinced nothing but scorn and derision towards black women in Africa and the Caribbean and ignored their presence in England. It seems clear that black men greatly outnumbered black women in England at the time. Contemporaries estimated the black population to number anything from 3,000 to 30,000 in the 1770s, depending on the context, and modern scholars put the true figure at about 10,000 — when the population of London was about half a million in all. This chapter attempts to give an impressionist overview of the lives of black women in London over a century, ending with an account of Mary Prince.

Black people had been brought to Britain as slaves from the sixteenth century and earlier. Grace Robinson is listed as a member of the Earl of Sackville's household in 1613.[1] As the plantation colonies of the Americas and the Caribbean developed so the black presence in England gradually became significant: returning planters, derided as *nouveaux riches*, merchants, slave traders, overseers and attorneys brought black slaves with them to Britain.

## Freedom strategies

Throughout this period black people, men as well as women, developed strategies to challenge their status as chattels and property and to obtain their freedom. These strategies included: being baptised; deserting their owners; seeking the intervention of sympathetic white people; and presenting petitions.

### Baptism

The law relating to slavery in England was uncertain during the seventeenth and early eighteenth century and there was a widespread belief that black people were slaves because they were heathens and that if they were baptised they became free. Black people brought cases before the courts in the hope of being declared legally free. For example, Katherine Auker petitioned the Court in 1690, saying that she had been baptised at St. Katherine's by the Tower. Her master and mistress had then 'tortured her and turned her out' and had her arrested and thrown in the Poultry Compter. Because her owners refused to give her a 'discharge' she could not be retained in service elsewhere. The Court ruled that she should be free to serve anyone until her master returned.[2]

The uncertainty in the law relating to slavery remained until 1729, when the Crown's Law Officers Sir Philip Yorke and Charles Talbot authoritatively ruled that a slave did not become free either by coming to Britain or Ireland or by being baptised. Despite this ruling, there remained a widespread belief that baptism made a slave free, a belief encouraged by a number of contradictory legal rulings in subsequent years. Hue and Cry notices from the early eighteenth century, offering rewards for the return of 'runaway slaves', men, women and children, suggest that black people claimed their freedom by deserting their owners.

In the 1760s, Granville Sharp, a clerk in the Ordnance Survey and later a key member of the Abolition movement[3] assisted several black slaves, Jonathon Strong, John and Mary Hylas, when asked to intervene on their behalf. As a result of this experience with black people, he set out to establish that slavery was contrary to English law. He succeeded in having the issue decided by the Courts in the case of James Somerset, who had been brought to Britain by his owner and later absconded. His owner re-captured him and intended to take him to Jamaica. The case came before the Court in 1771. After considerable delay Lord Mansfield gave his judgement, ruling that a slave could not be taken out of Britain against his will. However, Granville Sharp, the press, the pro-slavery lobby and

London's black community all believed that the judgement meant that all slaves became free once they reached England's free soil. Members of London's black community were in court to hear the judgement, and the *Public Advertiser* of 27 June 1772 reported that:

> On Monday near 200 Blacks, with their Ladies, had an Entertainment at a Public house in Westminster, to celebrate the Triumph which their Brother Somerset had obtained over Mr. Stuart his master. Lord Mansfield's health was echoed round the Room, and the Evening was concluded with a ball. The Tickets for admittance to this black Assembly were 5s. each.[4]

### The Somerset Myth

The Somerset judgement was understood to have freed black slaves once they were in Britain, though in law it did not do so. I shall refer to this as the 'Somerset myth', though I am mainly concerned to note its effects on black people and white. The judgement gave tremendous impetus to black people to free themselves and Granville Sharp continued to assist individual black people who sought his intervention. Writing to Dr Findlay in Glasgow shortly after the Somerset judgement, he records the story of Elizabeth Brooks:

> I have Original Letters by me wrote by a poor Negro woman, one Elizabeth Brooks, who after living nine or ten years with her Husband in a free state in London was found out by her Mistress (a West Indian Lady of Fortune in Cecil Street in the Strand), was torn by her from her afflicted and almost despairing Husband and secretly shipped for Antigua. This Lady also, it seems, is esteemed a *mighty good sort of Woman* in the Eyes of the World, but that did not prevent the ascendancy of her West Indian prejudices. She thought, perhaps, she had a *right* to do what she pleased with her *own property,* and, because she could not legally claim such property in England, she pretended that the poor Woman had carried away some of her Cloathes (the Old Gown upon her Back!) when she left her service, and by this means she obtained a warrant to throw the poor Woman into Gaol: and as soon as a ship was ready for Antigua she sent a Message to the Justice of the Peace signifying that she had Compassion for the poor Woman and therefore desired that she might be discharged, which was accordingly done; but when the poor Creature was returning home to her Husband she was waylaid by Order of her mistress, forced into a Post Chaise by an armed Ruffian, and hurried away to Gravesend where she was shipped for Antigua.[5]

Hannah More from Bristol had a similar story to tell Horace Walpole, towards the end of the century. A reward of a guinea was offered to anyone who could find a young black girl who had run away to avoid being returned to the Caribbean. Hannah More informed Walpole that she did not hear of the case until it was too late or she would have offered to buy the girl herself However, the girl had a luckier fate than might have been expected — some months later Hannah More wrote again to Walpole to inform him that the girl had escaped back to Bristol 'where those delightful people the Quakers who had been on the watch for her rescue, received her and got a warrant of protection, by which they keep her in defiance of all the human flesh merchants'.

Despite the fact that black people remained vulnerable to the danger of re-enslavement, the idea gained currency that Britain was 'free soil' for black people. Elizabeth Ann Miler came from Barbados to London in order to persuade her owners to free her. Her mother, called Old Doll, had been a privileged household slave on a plantation in Barbados owned by Mrs Newton, but believed that Mrs Newton had given her and her daughters their freedom before transferring the plantation to her cousins, John and Thomas Lane. The family adopted various tactics between 1790 and 1815 to be declared legally free. Old Doll and her daughters wrote to their owners in England asking them to honour the promise of Elizabeth Newton to free them. This had no effect. Elizabeth lost her privileged status as a household slave and was ordered to labour in the fields by the overseer, Mr Yard. During 1795-6 Elizabeth had been involved in considerable conflict with Mr Yard. He had beaten her and she had deserted the plantation, believing that he would kill her if she returned. She went first to the neighbouring island of St. Vincent and then to London, where she married a black man. Some time in 1796 she sought out Mr Lane and asked him to free her and her four children in Barbados. Thomas Lane wrote to his brother John and recorded the encounter thus:

> Eliz came again, and when I proposed her going back in a ship I had provided for she hesitated and at last desired we would give her liberty. I had a great deal of commotion with her. She was steady that she durst not go back to her former situation, for Yard would certainly kill her. If she was free, she could go back again and take care of her Child'n and all the slaves would be glad to hear the account she'd give them of our goodness to her and they would do their work cheerfully. In short she pleaded strongly for her liberty, with her little Girl in her arms.[6]

Elizabeth returned some while later to plead again for her freedom. Lane was unsure what to do. Again we see the Somerset myth being invoked:

> What can we do? We cannot compel her to go back — she *is* free, by setting her foot on English ground — I believe the Law is so. Therefore she is asking us to give her what she already has — Her Freedom and what we cannot take away from her.[7]

Having considered his rights and duties as a slave-owner, Lane then moved to a consideration of the financial implications, continuing:

> It will cost us 20 Guineas to send her back — If she goes as a free woman, I don't think we need be at that Expense. — But let her find her own way back as well as she can — Consider the whole of the case — we never sho'd have known anything of her if she had not come hither and told us who she is — our loss wou'd have been the same as it will be if we give her her freedom — and had we not better make a merit of necessity, & give her freedom? Let me hear from you. — The ship that wou'd have carried her from us sails on Tuesday or Wed'y at the furthest and she is to come to me again on Friday morning.[8]

The Lanes refused to give Elizabeth her freedom, but she did not give up. Six years later in 1801 she tried presenting a formal petition to Mr Lane in the hope of persuading him to reconsider his decision. The petition stated:

> The case and petition of Elizabeth Ann Miller, a free Black Woman from the Island of Barbados, is earnestly and humbly recommended to Mr Lane's humane attention and interposition. Her four children were seized as slaves during the life of Mrs Newton, by the then agent Mr Yard, and are still detained as such by Mr Lane's agent, Mr Wood; and have been, at different times, very severely ill-treated. Elizabeth Ann Miler came over to England six years ago, in the hopes of procuring an order from Mrs Newton for their release; but upon her arrival learnt that Mrs Newton had died just before. Elizabeth Ann Miller having therefore failed to accomplish her object, which brought her to England, and being most desirous of returning to her children in Barbados; most humbly solicits Mr Lane's goodness and Benevolence to grant her, under his hand, a certificate of her own freedom and an order upon his agent for the release of her children for which compassion and kindness towards her she will never cease, thro' life (as in duty bound) in fervent gratitude to pray. 6 May 25, 1801.[9]

Unfortunately it is not known if her petition was ever granted.

## Participation and interaction

Douglas Lorimer claims that black people began to free themselves during the period 1760 to 1790. I shall argue that there is evidence of black women living as free people throughout the eighteenth century. In my view, it was the Somerset case and the assistance of Granville Sharp which gave greater impetus to the formation of a free black community. This black community lived among, and as a part of, that section of society that contemporaries called 'the lower orders': people with a trade, people with none, labourers, street sellers and hawkers, ballad sellers, servants and prostitutes. Black women shared in the experiences of English women of a similar class, the large majority of whom were servants of various kinds, housemaids and laundry maids. They mixed with English servants as well as servants from India (known as Ayahs[10]), Ireland, Scotland, France and other European countries. Sir John Fielding, a magistrate and a hostile observer, author of *Penal Laws* (published in 1768, before the Somerset judgement) remarked that:

> Black servants no sooner arrive here than they put themselves on a footing with other servants, become intoxicated with liberty, grow refractory, and either by persuasion of others or from their own inclinations, begin to expect wages according to their own opinion of their merits; and as there are already a great number of black men and women who made themselves troublesome and dangerous to the families who have brought them over as to get themselves discharged, these enter into societies and make it their business to corrupt and dissatisfy the mind of every black servant who comes to England; first by getting them christened or married, which they inform them, makes them free.[11]

Black women who deserted their owners and attempted to live as free people found it very difficult to obtain wages, but there are certainly instances where they did so. There were black women who served an owner or employer for many years and were rewarded with legacies of property and often with their freedom. However, it was generally difficult for black women to obtain Poor Law relief, as they could not show a 'settlement' within a given parish. They received little assistance from the courts, as can be seen from the case of Charlotte Howe. She had been bought in America by a Captain Howe and came with him to Thames Ditton in 1781. He died in 1783 and she remained with his wife, who moved to Chelsea. She then went back to Thames Ditton, but was removed by the Poor Law Guardians to Chelsea. Her case came before the court in

1785 and was heard before Lord Mansfield, who commented that 'Where slaves have been brought here and have commenced actions for wages I have always nonsuited the plaintiff'. Not surprisingly, she lost her claim for Poor Law relief.

Black women were forced to rely on their own resourcefulness. There were few occupations open to women, white or black, and it was extremely difficult for black women to achieve a degree of economic independence. However, there are fleeting references to black women being engaged in a number of occupations, such as barmaid, publican and barber, as well as the most common occupation for women: servants. Advertisements for a position were placed in newspapers by servants of all nationalities who were without work, including black women.

Black women made the best of the limited opportunities open to them, which makes the story of one unnamed black woman all the more interesting. John Jackson, in *The History of the Scottish Stage* has a laugh at her expense as he records her efforts to obtain employment in the theatre. He recalls an incident in the 1780s when an agent goes to see a Mr Foote, a theatrical impresario, about an actress 'in praise of whose abilities he was not a little lavish'. However, the agent, in something of a fluster, says:

> Sir, there is one thing I had forgot to mention, and which you may possibly object to THE LADY IS A BLACK.'

To which Mr Foote replied: 'Oh! No matter, we shall introduce the Roman fashion: the lady shall wear a MASK'. Jackson noted that he had seen the same woman in Lancashire playing Polly in the Beggar's Opera, and that she had played Juliet in Romeo and Juliet a few nights earlier.[12]

A hundred years later, an article in *Notes and Queries* reviewed the history of black people on the stage in Britain. The writer on this occasion is far more sympathetic to this woman than Jackson had been, saving that:

> she had every qualification for the part save that of complexion. She was a negress. Like her gifted compatriot Ira Aldridge, she was devoured by a desire to shine in the classic drama; but, unfortunately, there are no female Othellos, no petticoated Oroonokos in our dramatic literature, so she was fain to fall back on Juliet, which, all things considered, she played respectably.[13]

## The Oldest Profession

For many women without work or an income there was no alternative to prostitution. Prostitution took many forms. Quite often women had other work and used prostitution as a means of supplementing their income. Patrick Colquhoun, in his *Treatise on the Police of the Metropolis*, estimated that there were 50,000 prostitutes in London, though modern scholars put the number nearer to 10,000.[14] Clearly a great many women had no other options open to them to survive. A few black women had some success catering to an upper class market of late eighteenth century rogues and rakes. The life of Black Harriet has been recorded in sufficient detail to give us an insight into the life of one black woman of the period, even though the account was written to titillate a male audience. We learn something of her background in Jamaica:

> She was purchased amongst other slaves when very young upon the Coast of Guinea, and carried to Jamaica where she was as usual put up to public sale, and purchased by a capital planter of Kingston. As she approached maturity, she discovered a lively genius, and a penetration far superior to the common run of Europeans, whose mind had been cultivated by learning. Her master now took particular notice of her, and removed her so far from her late menial capacity, as to make her a superintendent of the other female negroes. He gave Harriet a master to teach her to write, read, and so much of arithmetic as enabled her to keep the domestic accounts. He soon after distinguished her still farther from the rest of the slaves; he being a widower, used to frequently admit her to his bed: this honour was accompanied by presents which soon testified she was a great favourite, In this situation she remained for near three years, during which time she bore him two children.[15]

Then, she comes to England with her owner:

> His business calling him to England, Harriet accompanied him, and notwithstanding the Beauties of this island often attracted his attention, and he frequently gave a loose to his natural appetites with his own country-women, still she remained unrivalled on a constant flame. Nor was it, in some respect, extraordinary, for though her complexion might not be so engaging as that of the fair daughters of Albion, she had many allures that are not often met with in the female world who yield to prostitution. She was faithful to his bed, careful of his domestic concerns, exact in her accounts, and would not suffer any of the other servants to impose upon their master; and in this respect she favoured him some hundreds a year. Her person was very

alluring; she was tall, well made, and genteel; and since her arrival in England, she had given her mind to reading, and at her master's recommendation, perused several useful and entertaining books, calculated for women; whereby she had considerably improved her understanding, and had attained a degree of politeness scarce to be paralleled in an African female.[16]

After several months, her master died of smallpox and Harriet, like other black women in a similar position, was forced to rely on her own resources:

She had made some small provision for herself, with regard to clothes, and some trifling trinkets; but she had acted in so upright and generous a manner towards her departed master, that she had not amassed £5 in money, though she might easily, and without detection, have been the mistress of several hundreds. The scene was soon changed, and from being the superintendent of a noble table, she found herself reduced to a scanty pittance, and even that pittance could not last long, if she did not find some means of speedily recruiting her almost exhausted finances.[17]

Harriet, notwithstanding she had read some pious books, and many moral books found it necessary to make the most of her jetty charms, and accordingly applied to Lovejoy to be properly introduced into company. She was quite a new face, in every sense of the word, upon the Town, and a perfect phenomenon of her kind. He dispatched immediately a messenger to Lord S--- who instantly quitted the arms of Miss R---y for this black beauty.

Harriet was initially very successful, with well situated premises in Covent Garden. The account continues:

She resolved to vend her charms as dear as possible; and found that the caprice of mankind was so great, that she could command almost any price. In the course of a few months she could class among her list of admirers, at least a score of Peers and fifty Commoners, who never presented her with any thing less than soft paper commonly called a bank note.

Unfortunately things then went wrong for Harriet, partly because she gave up her business and partly because some of her fellow prostitutes took advantage of her:

Taking fancy to a certain officer of the Guards who had no more than his pay to subsist upon, she declined accepting the addresses of any of her admirers; and being at the same time obliged to dilate frequently her purse-strings in behalf of this Son of Mars, she soon found a great descalcation in the Rate of her receipts.

Also, she left her home in charge of servants, who ran up huge debts in fashionable shops which she could not pay. Harriet was imprisoned twice for debt, which broke her health and she died of tuberculosis in 1779.[18]

However, while Harriet may have been unusually gifted, she was by no means unique. *Harris' List of Covent Garden Ladies* (a list of prostitutes circulated to an upper class readership) lists Irish, Scottish, Jewish and English women, as well as black women. For the years 1788 to 1793 three black women are listed, including Eliza in 1789:

> Eliza is of dark complexion being a downright mulatto. She is somewhat addicted to swearing. She tells a good story, and can produce an excellent tale, which she charges little more for.[19]

In 1793 we read of Miss Wilson:

> The Island of Jamaica is the native soil of this wanton cyprian female, though she cannot boast of a complexion delicately fair, yet it must be acknowledged her features are very pleasing She is a girl of considerable taste and fashion; Covent Garden Theatre is her constant evening lounge, at which place she is known by many of gentlemen actors, one of which in the line is said to have been closely connected with her; report says she dances well, and her vocal abilities are of no inconsiderable promise, as she warbles with much sweetness and science; her conversation denotes her to be a girl of good sense.[20]

These women catered for the upper classes. There were many other women who served the multiracial communities in East London, which included the Irish communities of Whitechael and Spitalfields, and the Chinese and Indian seamen (known as Lascars) in Bethnal Green, Wapping, Shadwell and Poplar such a Black Sarah, who was featured in an issue of *The Town*, a two-penny news sheet, in 1839. She plied her trade along the Ratcliffe Highway in East London, where most of her customers were Chinese and Lascar seaman. The paper commented that she was a 'favourite to black and white'. It went on to describe how she walked the Highway with her friends Cocoa Bet, Bet Moses, the Mouth of the Nile, Salmony-faced Mary Anne, Peg Mitchell and others who formed a 'kind of convoy to her of the black flag' as they visited the public houses in the area.[21]

## Crime and Punishment

The communities of which black women became a part existed on the margins between respectability and crime. Criminal law in the eighteenth century resulted in thousands of people being transported for many different offences, including theft of relatively small sums. Studies of court records during the period 1780-1852 by Norma Myers and Ian Duffield reveal a small number of black women coming before the courts as defendants and also as victims and witnesses. Duffield found records of six women during the period 1812 to 1852, who were transported from places as far apart as Edinburgh, Dublin, London and Bristol, all of them found guilty of the theft, in some cases linked to prostitution. Three women, Marian Mitchell from Martinique, Elizabeth Jones from Mauritius and London-born Charlotte Clayton, were transported to Australia in the late 1830s.[22]

## Relative Privilege

There were a very small number of women who were more fortunate. The story of Elizabeth Belle Lindsay, called Dido (after the black Queen of Carthage, who delayed Aeneas on his way to founding Rome) has been told many times. Her father was Lord Mansfield's nephew and he had made her mother pregnant on a slave vessel. Dido lived with Lord Mansfield at Kenwood House on Hampstead Heath. She seems to have occupied a very ambivalent position in his family, Nonetheless, he provided her with a dowry when she married a Mr Davison. He left her a legacy of £500 and an annuity of £100 in his will. He also confirmed in his will that she was free.

Anne Sancho was the wife of Ignatius, who corresponded with literary figures such as Garrick and Sterne. His letters were published after his death to provide an income for her and their children.

A final example is Nico Strawbridge, mistress to George Bubb-Doddington, who was a friend of the Prince of Wales and was created Baron Melcombe in 1761. Nico was his mistress from 1730 to her death in 1742. Horace Walpole described her as 'a very handsome black woman'. Bubb-Doddington concealed from Nico that he was married. Bubb-Doddington is depicted in the Hogarth print of 1755 entitled 'Chairing the Member'.

## King and Country

I want to conclude this brief survey of some black women's lives by looking at three cases of participation by black women in English social and political life. Charlotte Gardner enters the historical record when she was charged with arson after the Gordon Riot of 1780 and was later hanged. The ostensible aim of the riot, named after Lord George Gordon, was to force the government to repeal a bill giving civil rights to Catholics, though historians such as George Rude argue that it was also an opportunity for the common people to settle old scores with the rich and powerful. That seemed to be true of Charlotte, as she and her friends 'pulled down' and burnt the house of a publican who had arranged for her friend to be evicted from her previous lodgings. The *Morning Chronicle* reported that 'The most remarkable trial was that of Mary Roberts and Charlotte Gardner, a Black, who were put to the bar, charged with being principally active in riotous proceedings...' Lettie Allen was called as a witness and stated that 'the black in particular called out frequently 'more wood, more wood for the fire".[23]

Economic opportunities for all women were, as I have indicated, limited and William Brown was one black woman who adopted a tactic employed by many women at the time to increase the opportunities open to them. Women who dressed as men could obtain work in occupations otherwise closed to them. Many served in the army and navy, others became pirates or highwaymen.[24] Moreover, a large but as yet un-quantified number of black men served in the British navy and army during this period. In an article entitled 'British Amazons' which described a number of women who had cross-dressed and served in the army and navy, Charles Dickens wrote about William Brown as follows:

> She can scarcely be called a British Amazon, unless her having served under the British flag entitled her to the designation. All we know about her is contained in this paragraph from the Annual Register of 1815: Amongst the crew of the Queen Charlotte, one hundred guns, recently paid off, it is now discovered was a female African, who had served as a seaman in the royal navy for upwards of eleven years, several of which she has been rated able on the books of the above ship, by the name of William Brown; she has served as captain of the foretop highly to the satisfaction of the officer. She is a smart figure, about five feet four inches in height, possessed of considerable strength and great activity; her features are rather handsome for a black, and she appears to be about twenty-six years of age. Her share of prize money is said to be considerable, respecting which she has

been several times within the last few days at Somerset-place. In her manners she exhibits all the traits of a British tar, and takes her grog with her late shipmates with the greatest gaiety. She says she is a married woman, and went to sea in consequence of a quarrel with her husband, who, it is said, has entered a caveat against her receiving her prize money. She declares her intention of again entering the service as a volunteer.[25]

Finally, there is the matter of political involvement. While there is no evidence of black women playing a leading role in the radical movements as Robert Wedderburn and William Davidson did, they were among the crowds that flocked to hear radical ideas, such as those of Robert Owen. Owenism was one of the first radical movements to allow women a public role. *Old England* reported in 1836 that:

> The last in the Course of Social Principles by Mrs Chappelsmith, late Miss Reynolds, was delivered on Tuesday night at the Lambeth Social Institute which, as usual, was attended by persons of both sexes, a motley company, exhibiting a great variety of dress and want of dress: coats of all colours, not excepting red, for there were soldiers present; hats of every shape, and no shape at all; rags and respectability; even black women were there, besides ancient dames of other hues who slept and snored at intervals, and young flames whose eyes knew no rest.[26]

## Black women, abolition and anti-slavery
### Sierra Leone

After the Somerset judgement of 1772, the black community is increasingly seen as a problem. The black community had been increased by the Black Loyalists from Nova Scotia, Canada, who came to London in the aftermath of the American War of Independence. They had fought for Britain during the war, in return for a promise of freedom. When the war ended they were evacuated to Nova Scotia and many then came to London. As many of them were literally destitute, a Committee for the Relief of the Black Poor was established which provided food and money to almost a thousand people.

The detailed background to the founding of the Sierra Leone colony and the role played by the Black Poor themselves is outside the scope of this chapter. However, in 1786, the Government was persuaded of the merits of a plan by Granville Sharp, Jonas Hanway and others to settle the Black Poor in Sierra Leone. In April 1787, 374 settlers sailed for Africa including 41 black women and 59 white women married to black men.

The colony was initially a failure and many of these settlers died. In 1799 it was re-established by the Black Loyalists from Nova Scotia, Canada, and run as a commercial venture by the Sierra Leone Company with a charter from Parliament. The colony was specifically intended to be a means by which the slave trade on the West Coast of Africa could be undermined.

The members of the Clapham Sect — Wilberforce and his circle of Evangelists in the Anglican Church — and the wider Abolition Movement were closely involved in the venture, providing both capital and support. They were keenly interested in the success of the colony and sponsored missionaries as well. The members of both the Clapham Sect[27] and the wider Abolition movement delighted in reading stories in missionary magazines of black people, men as well as women, living sober Christian lives. This is the background against which one should read the following account of Mary Perth, a black Loyalist from Nova Scotia who went to the colony in the 1790s. Reverend Clark, writing in *The Evangeline Magazine,* described her thus:

> There is one old woman the like of whom I have never talked with; she is more like one come down out of heaven to earth than like one who is preparing for glory.. . I blush in her presence and find I know nothing.

He went on to say that:

> I might have told you a great deal more about this good woman, this zealous and truly lively Christian; but have not time at present. On some future occasion, God willing, this I will do. I cannot conclude, however, without telling you that she was once a preacher in America.. I intend if she will allow me, to write a short account of her life, and send it home to be printed. I need not tell you that she is a black. This I can assure you is no hindrance to our Christian fellowship. I am as happy in her company, and in that of others as well, as ever I was in that of any Christian of my own colour.[28]

Mary Perth came to Britain in 1799 to look after some black children who were brought by Zachary Macauley (abolitionist, member of the Clapham Sect and Governor of the Colony) to England to be educated. She returned to Sierra Leone in 1801 when she married again in her sixties. I have included this brief passage about Mary Perth, as it illustrates the tendency of some missionaries to romanticise black women. This tendency would have unfortunate consequences later in the 1830s, as we shall see with another Mary.

## Anti-Slavery

In 1807 the Abolitionists achieved their aim and the slave trade was abolished. There was then a lull in Abolitionist activity until the 1820s when new campaigns by the Anti-Slavery Society were launched for improvement in the conditions of the slaves in the Caribbean. When reform seemed ineffective in improving the lives of the black slaves in the Caribbean and elsewhere, the Anti-Slavery Society campaigned for full emancipation. In the 1760s black people had turned to Granville Sharp for assistance and he personally helped hundred of black people. The Anti-Slavery Movement played a similar role in the 1820s. The Ladies Anti-Slavery Societies took a particular interest in black women, whom they portrayed as women doubly wronged, by both the Slave Trade itself and by the brutalities of plantation slavery, particularly the flogging and sexual abuse of black women. This is illustrated in a letter sent by Mary Capper to the Anti-Slavery Society in 1830 about a black woman living in Ramsgate, Kent, with a white woman from Trinidad who was a cruel and abusive owner. The white woman had sent for Polly as, allegedly, no English servant would work for her. Polly had asked a Methodist minister to baptise her. Mary Capper met Polly and seeing that she was ill-treated decided to help her if she could. It is noteworthy that both Polly and Mary Capper start from the premise that she (Polly) was free in England:

> Polly told me that she knew she was free in England, but she thought she was more a slave than in the West Indies, as she had none of her acquaintances to speak to, that she should like very much to live in an English family, but that her mistress told her the English looked upon blacks as dogs, and would not think of letting her serve them. I told her I had many fiends much interested about the Black People, that I would endeavour to find her a situation amongst them, and would send for her again.[29]

And so Mary Capper decided to hire Polly as a servant for her own family and called at the house to collect her. The white woman threw Polly out when she realised the purpose of Mary Capper's visit, and she continues her letter with a few words about the exchange between them:

> When her mistress found Polly immediately determined to accept my offer, she said much against her and told her she should go *immediately,* as she would not keep such an ungrateful wretch in her house. The haughty and brutal manner in which she spoke to her gave me a deeper idea of slavery than I had ever before had.

Polly was then employed by Mary Capper as a servant but still she felt the pain of all the other enslaved black people:

> ...I noticed her frequently dejected and sometimes her in tears. Upon my asking her the occasion of this she told me 'nothing the matter mistress, nothing the matter — only when I think of my people, my heart is full and the water will come to my eyes.'

Mary Capper was a friend of Hannah Kilham who was something of an expert on African languages (mainly for the purpose of translating the bible), and identified Polly's language as Twi. They were interested that Polly had direct experience of the slave trade: 'I found from herself that she clearly remembered being stolen; that she was gathering shells on the sea shore, under the direction of her grandfather, when some black men caught her, and put her in a sack...'

The members of the Clapham Sect were principally concerned with conversion, both of the working classes in England and of the 'heathen' elsewhere. They sponsored bible societies and missionary societies, published tracts, handbooks, and didactic novels of all kinds. They would have been delighted to see Polly come to a knowledge of 'true religion'. Mary Capper concludes her letter by enthusing that::

> As soon as she was at ease with her fellow servants, she said to one of them very earnestly 'do tell me whether I have a soul, for my mistress in Ramsgate says I have no soul, that the Almighty has no more to do with Black people than with dogs.' She had such pleasure in attending a place of worship, but more still in hearing the Bible and serious books read to her.[30]

Elizabeth Dudley, who was also involved in the Anti-Slavery Movement, wrote to the Society about another black woman, whom she does not name in her letter, in order to seek funds to assist her:

> Having understood that the meeting for suffering has some funds available for Anti-Slavery purposes, I hope it may not be deemed improper of me to present a claim on behalf of a black girl recently brought from Buenos Ayres who was given up by her mistress at the request of a few friends. She has been placed at the Borough Road School where there is reason to hope that she will receive such instruction as may fit her for becoming useful to some of her injured fellow sufferers in Africa or elsewhere.

The letter continues with a reference to the Somerset myth, relating that the girl had been given as a present to an Admiral's daughter as a present:

but being often very cruelly treated was rejoiced to hear from the sailors on shipboard that she would be free on reaching England where she arrived only about three days ago, when her case became known to some benevolent persons in Southampton.[31]

It was the case of Grace Jones in 1822 which first began to cast doubt on whether the Somerset judgement had in fact freed the black slaves in England. Grace Jones had come to England with her owner from Antigua and lived with her for several years. The owner then decided to return to Antigua and Grace Jones returned with her on the understanding that she would be freed on arrival there. However, the owner, reneged on that promise and when they arrived in Antigua was prosecuted for illegally importing a slave. The Anti-slavery campaigners were as keen as the Government that the case should be heard on appeal in England so that an authoritative ruling could be given. Lord Stowell, who heard the case, refused to hear evidence that Grace Jones had been kidnapped and ruled that a period of residence in England 'suspends' but does not extinguish the slave condition. The judgement was met with relief by the West Indian Planters and with dismay by the Anti-Slavery Movement and more radical opinion such as the *New Times,* which declared that:

> The female in question was not a voluntary agent in the re-imposition of her chains; she was *kidnapped* and a criminal indictment may as legally be preferred against those who induced her to quit England, as if she had been a white native of this island. If her mistress had told the female that by her residence in Antigua she would again be subject to the shackles from which her residence in freed her, is it probable, is it credible — that she would have accompanied her?[32]

## Mary Prince

It seems to me that there were several black communities in London, which may well have had very little contact with each other. On the one hand there were the black people who, as we have seen, became part of the lower orders or, as the nineteenth century progressed, the working-class, and who lived in St Giles, Seven Dials, Holborn and parishes to the east of the Thames: Bethnal Green, Wapping, Shadwell. On the other hand, there were the servants of white West Indians — planters, attorneys and others — who continued to bring black people to Britain as slaves throughout the 1820s, and lived in affluent parts of London: the City itself, and suburbs such as Clapham, Clapton, Greenwich and Tottenham.

I want to conclude with a brief look at *The History of Mary Prince, a West Indian Slave, Related by Herself,* since it effectively draws together the themes raised in this chapter: freedom, economic independence for women, and inter-racial friendship. Mary Prince was born in Turks Island in 1788. Over the next forty years she was owned by a number of cruel and abusive owners at whose hands she frequently suffered violent physical assault. In the years immediately before she came to England, she had been a domestic slave to a Mr and Mrs Wood from Antigua. They were frequently violent and abusive, and after many years of overwork and abuse at their hands, Mary became increasingly disabled by rheumatism. During the time that she was owned by the Woods, she became a member of the Moravian Church, and married a free black man, Daniel James.

In about 1828 when Mary Prince was about forty, she came with her owners to England. They intended to put their son in school and take their daughters home. It was not unusual for household slaves to accompany their owners on visits to England and Mary Prince's owners continued to expect her to wash stacks of laundry, which her disabilities made painful and difficult. Eventually, unable to suffer the abuse any longer, Mary Prince decided to embark on an uncertain freedom. Eventually she found her way to the Anti-Slavery Society and told her story to its secretary, Thomas Pringle, who agreed to employ her as a servant. While she was employed by him she 'related' her autobiography to Susannah Strickland and other women involved in the Anti-Slavery Movement and this was subsequently published as an anti-slavery tract.

It is significant that Mary 'related' rather than wrote the History, but nonetheless, as a black woman she was exceptional in achieving this measure of self-expression, although her History was censored in certain crucial ways. During the time that Mary Prince was owned by Mr and Mrs Wood she still hoped to be freed and reunited with her husband in Antigua. She expressed her dilemma thus: 'I knew that I was free in England, but I did not know where to go, or how to get my living, and therefore I did not like to leave the house'.[33] So she put her trust in Providence and turned to Mr and Mrs Mash, an English couple employed by Mrs Wood, for help. She lived with them for some time and they cared for her while she was sick with rheumatism. They were also instrumental in helping her find the Moravian community in London (the missionary society that she was acquainted with in Antigua). The Moravians told her about the Anti-Slavery Society and she called at their offices to see if they could find a way for her to be freed and to return to Antigua. They sought legal advice and concluded that while Mary was free in England, nothing could make her free in the West Indies. They tried to persuade Mr Wood to allow her to purchase her freedom but he refused. She also presented a petition to Parliament, but this was ordered to 'lie upon the table'.[34]

Although there is no further record of Mary Prince, her *History* was the focus of controversy between the pro- and anti-slavery lobbies in the final year or two of slavery. The pro-slavery lobby in England, led by James McQueen (Editor of the *Glasgow Courier)* and others, made determined efforts to discredit it. Despite Pringle's best efforts to avoid giving offence and to verify the accuracy of every detail in The *History,* two bitterly critical articles appeared in the press. The first, published in the *Bermuda Royal Gazette* in November 1831, was entitled 'The Anti-Slavery Society and the West India Colonists'. The article declared that Mary Prince is 'falsely designated a West India Slave but is in fact a free woman living in London'. The writer then proceeds to deny the truth of Mary Prince's allegations of ill-treatment and flogging, supporting Mr Wood by asserting that he had:

> most justly refused to be ensnared in the trap laid for him, to induce him to sell the freedom of Mary Prince as she is already at liberty in England; and who, if Mr Wood were to treat as a slave would subject himself to the penalties of an act of Parliament which contains a special clause against such proceeding.[35]

And the final insult, hurled at both Mary Prince and Thomas Pringle, is that he 'sees nothing but purity in a prostitute because she knew how and when to utter the name of the Deity, to turn up the whites of her eyes and to make a perfect mockery of religion'.

The second article, by James McQueen, a notorious polemicist and pro-slavery writer, was published in *Blackwood's Edinburgh Magazine* in the same month, and was far more wide-reaching. It took the form of an open letter to Earl Grey, the Colonial Secretary, and as such responsible for the West Indian colonies and government policy on slavery. McQueen, too, distorts the facts of Mary Prince's experiences in England and in the West Indies, deriding them as her 'washing tub tales'. He gathers together letters from Mr Wood's colonial cronies in the West Indies, some free black women in Antigua and her husband. They all stated that her allegations of cruelty were untrue, and strongly implied that she made money by prostitution. As for Pringle, McQueen hints that his motive for letting Mary Prince tell her *History* in his parlour (to his female relatives) was sexual. As he put it 'In London maidservants are not removed from the washing-tub to the parlour without an object'[36].

The controversy surrounding The *History,* and the attempt to discredit it, led to two libel actions. Pringle had attempted to check every fact and detail in The *History,* and to ensure that no unacceptable personal details about Mary Prince were included in it. However, as the pro-slavery lobby took steps to discredit the *History,* a number of issues about Mary Prince's past were revealed, of which the most embarrassing to Thomas Pringle and the Anti-Slavery Society was that she had lived with a white Captain for seven years before her marriage.

There is no further record of Mary Prince and one wonders if she ever went back to Antigua, particularly as the pro-slavery lobby had persuaded her husband to give witness against her. In his supplement to the *History,* Pringle drew connections between Mary Prince, Grace Jones and other black people brought to Britain in similar circumstances. He concluded the *History* with a plea that Parliament should enact a law to confirm that all black slaves brought to England with their owners' consent were free and thus:

> to declare in the most ample sense of the words (what we had long fondly believed to be the fact, though it now appears that we have been mistaken) THAT NO SLAVE CAN EXIST WITHIN THE SHORES OF GREAT BRITAIN.[37]

## Conclusion

In this paper the relatively few black women who found their way into the historical record have been called upon to speak for the many black women of whom we have no record. I hope that I have given an indication of the diversity of the lives of black women during this period — women who, above all, were individuals and whose strength of character shines through the sketchy and incomplete records available to us.

## Further reading

Fryer, P: *Staying Power: The History of Black People in Britain*, London, Pluto Press, 1984

Gerzina, G: *Black England*, London, John Murray,1995

Killingray, D (ed): *Africans in Britain*, London, Cass, 1994

Shyllon, F: *Black Slaves in Britain London*, Published by Oxford University Press for the Institute of Race Relations, 1974

Shyllon, F: *Black People in Britain, 1555-1860,* London, Oxford University Press for the Institute of Race Relations, 1977

Walvin, J: *The Black Presence*, London, Orbach and Chambers, 1971

Walvin, J: *Black and White*, London, Allen Lane, the Penguin Press, 1973

## Notes

1.  Sackville West, V: *Knole and the Sackvilles*. Heinemann, London, 1922, p191. Also referred to in Fryer P., *Staying Power,* Pluto Press, London, 1984, p24.
2.  George, M. D: *London Life in the Eighteenth Century,* Penguin, London 1925, p.141.
3.  I use the term 'Abolition movement' to describe the campaign against the slave trade from the 1770s to1807 when the Britain outlawed the slave trade
4.  *The Public Advertiser* 27 June 1772
5.  Granville Sharp Letter Book in York Minister Library
6.  Newton Plantation Papers, Senate House Library, University of London. See m23 series. The papers are referred to in Beckles H. McD., *Natural Rebels* Zed Press London 1989.
7.  Ibid
8.  Ibid
9.  Ibid
10. I am mainly concerned with women of African descent in this chapter. However, it should be noted that contemporaries referred to Indians as 'East India Blacks' to distinguish them from 'West India Blacks'. Their numbers in England were relatively small during this period, though it increased during the course of the nineteenth century. For further information about the Ayahs see Visram R., *Ayahs, Lascars and Princes,* Pluto Press, London, 1986.
11. Sir John Fielding Penal Laws quoted in George op cit. p.140.
12. Jackson, J: *History of the Scottish Stage from its first establishment to the present time, with a distinct narrative of some recent theatrical transactions,* Edinburgh, 1793.
13. An article entitled 'First Real Negro on the Stage' in *Notes and Queries* 31 August 1899 second series.
14. Porter, R., and Lesley, H., *Facts of Life,* Yale University Press, London, 1995
15. *Nocturnal Revels: or The History of King's Place, and other Modern Nunneries.* second edition, M Goadby, volume II, London 1779, pp.98-102.
16. Ibid
17. Ibid
18. Ibid
19. *Harris' List of Covent Garden Ladies.... for the year 1788*
20. *Harris' List of Covent Garden Ladies.... for the year 1793*

21. *The Town* (two-penny newsheet), 1839.
22. Killingray, D: *Africans in Britain,* Cass, London, 1994.
23.  See for example Wilkinson, G. T: *The Newgate Calender* originally published in 1828 and reprinted in 1991 by Cardinal with an introduction by C. Hibbert. And also *Morning Chronicle* 4-7 July 1780.
24. See Wheelwright J: *Amazons and Military Maids,* Pandora Press, London 1989.
25. Dickens C: *All Year Round,* 6 April 1872. I am grateful to Julie Wheelwright for this reference.
26. *Old England,* 26 October 1836
27. By which I mean Wilberforce and his circle of friends, who were Evangicals in the Anglican Chruch.
28. An article entitled 'Singular Piety in an African Female' by Reverend Mr Clark in *The Evangeline Magazine* Volume IV, 1796 pp. 460-463
29. Letter from Mary Capper in the Friends House Library. Anti-Slavery Correspondence 18211832. temp mss 101/3. I am grateful to Clare Midgley for this reference.
30. Ibid
31. Ibid
32. *New Times,* 9 November 1827
33. Ibid p.78.
34. Ibid p.117
35. *Bermuda Royal Gazette* 'The Anti Slavery Society, and the West India Colonists' 22 November 1831
36. *Blackwood's Edinburgh Magazine,* November 1831.
37. *The History* p.115

# 4

# 'Remember Those in Bonds, As Bound with Them':
## Women's approach to anti-slavery campaigning in Britain 1780-1870

*Clare Midgley*

The exhortation by nineteenth century women anti-slavery campaigners to "remember those in bonds, as bound with them' has been lost to historical memory.[1] Until recently little research was conducted into the lives and resistance of enslaved women in the British West Indies or into the involvement of women in the anti-slavery campaign in Britain.[2] In this chapter I contribute to the second half of the process of recollection, through describing and discussing the distinctive contributions which women made to the organisation, activities and ideology of the British anti-slavery movement.[3]

A study of women anti-slavery campaigners is, I believe, of significance to feminists today because it provides a way of addressing important questions concerning the historical relationship between black women and white, and between the politics of gender and the politics of race and class.[4] This project is partly inspired by black feminist criticisms of white feminists for our unquestioning celebration of a universal 'sisterhood' of women and our failure to challenge racism and class oppression in tandem with sexism.[5]

The chapter begins with a chronological overview of women's contributions to successive anti-slavery campaigns in Britain. There follows a discussion of the backgrounds of women activists, and an exploration of their motivations. This leads to an examination of the development of a distinctive female anti-slavery perspective which focused on concern for enslaved women. Finally, I make some comments on the links between abolitionism and the development of feminism, and suggest the value of an understanding of anti-slavery history to feminists today.

Campaigning against the slave system in Britain passed through several overlapping stages. Firstly, there was the question of slavery within Britain itself: individual black men and women who were brought to Britain by their owners. Their own resistance to their chattel status is explored by Joan Grant in an earlier chapter. It was their position that led to the first white action against slavery: Granville Sharpe's attempts to get slavery in England made illegal through a series of court rulings.[6]

The beginnings of an organised campaign by white abolitionists came in 1783, when Quakers decided to organise committees to petition Parliament against the slave trade. This trade was on a massive scale: between 1562 and 1807 British ships, based in ports like Liverpool, Bristol, Hull and Glasgow, were responsible for the transportation of some two to three million African men, women and children to the Americas. Packed like sardines into the ships, many died en route. Following the example of Spain and Portugal, Britain created a 'triangular trade' involving the exchange of home manufactured goods for slaves in Africa, the exchange of these slaves for colonial produce, and the sale of this slave-grown produce — particularly sugar — in Britain. The relegation of human beings to chattels involved in this trade is brought home by documents such as a 'sale of goods' from Sierra Leone which records the exchange of a woman slave for one piece of planes, seven 771b kettles, 3 pieces of chintz and one piece of handkerchief stuff.[7]

The Quaker abolition committee was followed in 1787 by the formation of the non-sectarian Society for the Abolition of the Slave Trade. The group set an organisational pattern which was to be followed by subsequent national organisations: it had an all-male national committee which met in London and kept in close contact with the male Parliamentary leaders of the campaign, and a series of local societies affiliated to it. Women were involved in several ways. Some were the wives and daughters who formed the female support network behind the male leadership. Some, like Lady Middleton (d. 1792), attempted to use their high social standing to exert influence on politicians.[8] Others subscribed to the national society or to its local groups — 206 women made up approximately 10 per cent of total subscribers to the national society in 1788, a considerable number given that the majority of women did not possess an independent income. In Manchester the largest, most active and most radical local society issued a public appeal to the 'most amiable Part of the Creation' and recruited 68 female subscribers, nearly a quarter of the total membership of 302.[9]

Many women in Manchester and elsewhere joined in the boycott of slave-grown produce, responding to appeals such as that of the Irish Quaker poet Mary Birkett to 'no more the blood-stain'd lux'ry choose'.[10] This 'abstention' or 'antisaccharite' campaign, which has parallels to the recent anti-apartheid boycott of South African goods involved women using their domestic role as household purchasers for a political end. On the basis of an extensive tour of England in 1791, the leading abolitionist Thomas Clarkson estimated that some three hundred thousand persons in England and Wales were abstaining from the use of West Indian sugar, and around half of these were probably female, since boycotts tended to occur on a household basis.[11]

Another characteristic of the abolition campaign at this period was an outpouring of sentimental anti-slavery poems, which gained wide circulation through publication in periodicals and newspapers.[12] Many of these verses were written by women, ranging from schoolgirl amateurs to well-known professional writers like Hannah More (1745-1833), whose poem *Slavery* (1788) was written explicitly as propaganda to aid William Wilberforce at his opening of the parliamentary campaign against the slave trade.[13] The earliest British anti-slavery novel, Aphra Benn's *Oroonoko*, (1688) was revived in play form and attracted large audiences around the country; in Manchester a special prologue was added, praising women's anti-slavery work.[14]

As a result of social restrictions on women's public and political activities at the period it was unusual for women to express their opposition to slavery through writing political pamphlets, signing petitions or public speaking. However, there were exceptions: leading radical women Mary Wollstonecraft (1759-1797) and Helen Maria Williams (1762?-1827) opposed slavery in books that argued for the 'rights of man'; women very occasionally signed anti-slavery petitions;

and in at least two instances women gave public lectures against the slave trade in commercially-run London debating clubs.[15]

There was a lull in the popular anti-slavery campaign between the passage in 1807 of the Act abolishing the British slave trade and the inauguration in 1823 of a campaign directed against slavery itself. This new campaign was motivated by the realisation that, despite the abolition of the slave trade, conditions had not improved for slaves in the British colonies in the West Indies. Life for black men, women and children on the plantations, where sugar was the main crop, was characterised by unremitting physical toil, frequent punishments, and sufferings from disease. Of those Africans strong enough to survive the 'Middle Passage', up to a third died within a year or two of their arrival in the West Indies.[16]

The campaign against this system of extreme exploitation was co-ordinated by the Anti-Slavery Society and initially aimed at the mitigation and gradual abolition of slavery. While women continued during this period to be excluded from the central national committee, their activities were now transformed from individual support to organised campaigning through the network of local ladies' anti-slavery associations. This development was encouraged by the majority of the male leadership despite opposition from William Wilberforce, who disapproved of 'proceedings unsuited to the female character as delineated in scripture".[17]

By 1831 there were at least thirty-nine ladies' associations, the larger with several hundred subscribers, covering most English counties, as well as one group in Wales, one in Scotland and one in Ireland. The societies were based in a wide variety of locations, from small market towns to large industrial cities. Although there were about twice as many men's groups, many women's groups were in towns with no corresponding men's auxiliary.[18]

Even when they were in the same location, ladies' associations almost all operated independently of the local men's group. In this they differed from the pattern of the Bible Society and most other philanthropic organisations of the period, in which women's groups tended to be auxiliary to local men's societies.[19] Indeed, there is evidence that this pattern of sex-segregated organisation, which was to remain the norm throughout the duration of the anti-slavery movement, afforded women's groups considerable autonomy.

The most striking example of female organisational autonomy is provided by the Birmingham-based Ladies' Society for the Relief of Negro Slaves. This society was formed in April 1825 as an independent group rather than an auxiliary of the Anti-Slavery Society, and it acted as national coordinator and promoter of female organisations rather than as a typical local group. Its founders and co-secretaries were two philanthropic local women: Mary Lloyd (1795-1868), wife of a Quaker industrialist, and Lucy Townsend (d.1847), wife of an Evangelical clergyman. The Birmingham society oversaw a network of local district treasurers which by 1830 numbered forty-nine women, spread over England, as well as individuals in Wales and Dublin and as far afield as France, the Cape of Good Hope, Sierra Leone and Calcutta. These women collected subscriptions and distributed propaganda produced by the Birmingham society, including anti-slavery albums and handsewn work-bags containing collections of pamphlets and engravings. In some cases they also established local societies, which maintained close contacts with Birmingham. The importance of the Birmingham society is suggested by its income of £908 in 1826, which compares to the national Anti-Slavery Society's total income of £2933 for that year. The women's group regularly received subscriptions from two to three hundred women and donations from over a hundred more.[20]

The activities of men's and women's groups both overlapped and complemented each other. Both groups prioritised the diffusion of information and the arousal of public opinion against slavery. Men's groups, however, tended to go about this through organising public meetings, women through door-to-door canvassing. Both groups collected subscriptions and donations, which they used partly to fund their own activities and partly to donate to the national Anti-Slavery Society. Women, however, were more successful fund-raisers than men, and by 1829, despite their smaller number, ladies' associations were contributing considerably more than men's societies to national Anti-Slavery Society coffers.[21] In addition, as 'negroes' friend' societies, women's groups commonly donated to groups involved in the practical aid, education and religious conversion of black people in the West Indies. They thus combined support for anti-slavery with support for missions and education whereas men's groups tended to support these different objectives through separate organisations. Another differing emphasis was that men's societies took the lead in petitioning Parliament whereas women's groups led the organisation of the systematic boycott of slave-grown produce, visiting every household in several cities to promote abstention.[22]

At this period women were active not only as organisers and canvassers but also as authors of anti-slavery propaganda. Many ladies' associations produced printed annual reports of their activities for their members, and extracts from these appeared in local newspapers and national periodicals. Women also wrote anti-slavery pamphlets, many of them aimed specifically at a female audience, others at the concerned public in general. One of these, *The History of Mary Prince*, an autobiography told by an enslaved woman brought by her mistress from the West Indies to Britain, was intended to 'let English people know the truth' about slavery so 'that they may break our chains, and set us free'.[23]

The most controversial anti-slavery pamphlet of the period was *Immediate, not Gradual Abolition*, written by a Quaker woman from Leicester, Elizabeth Heyrick. In this Heyrick appealed to women to organise the slave sugar boycott as the best way of bringing down slavery in the face of the inevitable failure of the 'worldly politicians', whose policy of amelioration and gradual abolition had 'converted the great business of emancipation into the object under political consideration' and thus 'withdrawn it from divine, and placed it under human patronage'. Her passionate and well-reasoned call for the immediate, unconditional emancipation of slaves gained support from several women's groups and set in motion a debate among abolitionists which was to lead in 1830-31 to a change to an immediatist policy by the national leadership. [24]

The year 1830 saw a general increase in the intensity of anti-slavery campaigning. An important development of the period was the employment of paid travelling lecturers, or agents, by the national society. This scheme had been initiated by the Female Society for Birmingham in conjunction with the Dublin Negroes' Friend Society, and was greeted enthusiastically by ladies' associations: in its first year the Agency Committee of the Anti-Slavery Society received 320 invitations from women's groups compared to only nine from men's auxiliaries.[25]

These agents stimulated a popular nation-wide campaign centering on the mass petitioning of Parliament. Women now began to organise their own petitions as well as signing some of the general petitions from local communities and congregations. Thirty-four female petitions against slavery were presented to the House of Commons in 1830-31, and a further 105 in the first half of 1833, when women formed around one third of total signatories to anti-slavery petitions.[26] Most impressive was the massive national female anti-slavery petition of 1833, organised by the London Female Anti-Slavery Society. Described at the time as a 'huge featherbed of a petition' its 187,157 signatures were collected within only ten days and had to be hauled into Parliament by four men (women not being allowed onto the floor of the House of Commons).[27] This mass petitioning marks the first largescale attempt by women to directly influence Parliamentary politics. As such, it needs to be restored to its key place in women's history. It was the result of female initiatives, condoned rather than actively encouraged by male abolitionists and religious leaders.

The Emancipation Act of 1833 was not viewed as a complete success by many abolitionists. When it came into force on 1st August 1834 it did not immediately free slave men and women, but instead introduced a transitional apprenticeship system. This required all slaves over six years of age to continue working unpaid for their former owners — until 1840 in the case of agricultural workers, and 1838 for others. Concern about the continuance of terrible physical punishments under this system was aroused in part by accounts received from missionaries and teachers in the West Indies. Many of these letters were sent directly to ladies' anti-slavery associations, which were heavily involved in financing educational work.[28] Resulting public concern led to the launching in 1837 of a popular campaign against apprenticeship at a meeting in Exeter Hall in London. At this meeting 'the ladies formed a very considerable portion, if not an actual majority, of the audience', and women immediately began amassing signatures to a national female anti-apprenticeship address to the newly ascended Queen Victoria. A staggering 449,540 signatures were collected for the petition, and separate addresses from Scotland and Ireland bore 135,083 and 77,000 signatories respectively.[29] The total number of signatories exceeded those collected by women in 1833 and was, in the words of a contemporary anti-slavery paper, 'wholly unprecedented ... in the annals of petitioning'. [30]

With full emancipation in 1838 women did not give up interest in anti-slavery but rather turned their attention to 'universal abolition' and, together with male abolitionists, became involved in campaigns against the participation of other European powers in the African slave trade, against the continuance of so-called 'native' slavery in British India, and, most long-lastingly, against slavery in the United States. Women were involved in this work through the network of ladies' associations linked to the new national society, the British and Foreign Anti-Slavery Society (which persists to this day as the Anti-Slavery Society). They also ran some of the most active independent local societies: groups like the Edinburgh Ladies' Emancipation Society, run by Quakers Jane and Eliza Wigham; and the Bristol and Clifton Ladies' Anti-Slavery Society, led by

Mary Estlin, a Unitarian radical who persuaded the society to sever its links with the conservative national society publicly.[31] Such independent groups tended to align themselves with the radical 'Garrisonian' wing of the American anti-slavery movement, which had strong links to the developing women's rights movement. They became embroiled in the controversies over ideology and tactics which deeply split the transatlantic movement in the 1840s and 1850s. These controversies first became public in Britain at the World Anti-Slavery Convention in London in 1840, at which the male leadership of the British movement, aligning itself with the more conservative wing of American abolitionism, refused to accept the credentials of women delegates appointed by American 'Garrisonian' societies.[32]

Ladies' anti-slavery associations, fewer in number than men's societies in the 1820s and 1830s, had by the late 1840s and 1850s become both numerically predominant and in many cases more active than men's groups.[33] This was partly because men lost interest in a cause which had become politically marginal within Britain itself, partly because those areas of campaigning appropriate to combating foreign slavery were those in which women had the traditional expertise: the slave-produce boycott, fund-raising, and moral pressure. Anna Richardson, a Quaker activist from Newcastle-upon-Tyne, co-ordinated the boycott of American slave-grown cotton; national networks of women collected fancy goods for the bazaars which were one of the major sources of funding for rival American anti-slavery factions; and the Duchess of Sutherland's fashionable London circle was responsible for the largest British moral protest against slavery, the Stafford House Address of 1853.[34]

The 1840s and 1850s was a period of close transatlantic contacts among abolitionists. African-American fugitive slaves included Ellen Craft (1826-90), who disguised herself as a white man in order to escape from slavery and fled with her husband to Britain. Such fugitives joined the anti-slavery movement.[35] An English woman, Julia Griffiths, travelled to the United States and became personal assistant to leading African-American abolitionist, Frederick Douglass, then returned to Britain and formed a network of ladies' associations to provide financial support for his work.[36] Many other British women cultivated strong links and friendships with leading American abolitionists, with whom they exchanged views on a wide range of reform and political issues including feminism and pacifism as well as abolition.[37]

Partly as the result of stimulus from their American sisters, during the 1850s a minority of British women pushed for more equal participation in the anti-slavery movement. The Leeds Anti-Slavery Association, founded in 1853 to exploit popular anti-slavery sentiment aroused by Harriet Beecher Stowe's best-selling novel *Uncle Tom's Cabin*, broke with the convention of separatist organisation by having both male and female officers and members.[38]

The following year, spurred by Harriet Lupton, a Unitarian radical and supporter of women's rights who had been instrumental in forming the Leeds society, two Manchester women presented themselves as delegates at a national anti-slavery conference in London. Rebecca Whitelegge and her co-worker Rebecca Moore, an Irish Quaker who was later to become active in the women's suffrage movement, had their credentials accepted by the male organisers, finally breaking the ban on women delegates which had been enforced at the World Anti-Slavery Convention in London in 1840.[39] Further progress was made in 1859-60, when African-American abolitionist Sarah Parker Remond (1826-1894) became the first woman to conduct an anti-slavery public lecture tour of England, Scotland and Ireland.[40] She also joined the London Emancipation Committee, a short-lived anti-slavery radical group formed in 1859 of both male and female, black and white and British and American members.[41]

During the American Civil War in 1861-5 women continued to be active. Harriet Martineau, best known as the author of popular works on political economy, brought her journalistic skills to bear on drumming up support for the North on the grounds that slavery was 'the great question which underlies the whole quarrel', in a series of influential leaders for the *Daily News*.[42] Other women got involved in practical aid to newly freed slaves, collecting funds and organising sewing circles to make clothing for the destitute, and members of the Ladies' London Emancipation Society produced a series of pamphlets condemning the southern slave system.[43]

The freedmen's aid societies were disbanded in 1868, but some women continued to take an interest in issues of slavery and the fate of the freedmen. The Birmingham Ladies' Negro's Friend Society, founded in 1825, continued to meet until 1919, by which time some of its officers were descendants of its original members.

It is clear, then, that women made important and distinctive contributions to the anti-slavery movement in Britain. These campaigners came to the anti-slavery cause from a range of backgrounds and for a variety of reasons, bringing different perspectives and levels of commitment and becoming involved in diverse ways. Perhaps the most fundamental division was between those women who were members of local ladies' anti-slavery associations, and the wider female public whose support these activists enlisted on specific occasions and for particular aspects of their campaigns.

The individuals about whom most information is available are the officers and committee members of ladies' associations, who formed the female organisational leadership. These women can be categorised as middle-class in terms of their family backgrounds: most did not undertake waged work, but were the wives and daughters of clergymen and ministers, of comfortably-off local businessmen or of wealthy industrialists, merchants and bankers. Some lived in large industrial centres like Birmingham, Glasgow and Manchester, others in small local market towns. They were generally either Evangelical Anglican or Nonconformist in religious denomination, with Quakers predominating. They came from similar backgrounds to leading male activists, and family connections, which frequently followed denominational lines, were vitally important to the anti-slavery network.

The differing contributions made by male and female family members to the anti-slavery movement illuminate the restrictions under which women laboured. Joseph Sturge of Birmingham, leader of the British and Foreign Anti-Slavery Society, lived with his sister Sophia, on whose advice and support he placed great reliance; but Sophia herself, active in the Birmingham Ladies' Negro's Friend Society, local women's society, was excluded from the national decision-making of the movement because she was a woman.[44] Similarly, Joseph Pease, leader of the British India Society, depended on the full-time voluntary work of his daughter Elizabeth (1807-97), but she was assigned no formal post in the Society.[45] Mary Estlin, who in the 1850s worked closely with her father, John Bishop Estlin in support of the radical 'Garrisonian' abolitionists, became discouraged when her father and his colleagues 'took no account' of a major policy initiative which she proposed.[46]

Women's activism was also hampered by domestic responsibilities. Married women like Lucy Townsend, a vicar's wife with ten children, and her co-worker Mary Lloyd, wife of a colliery and foundry owner, had to fit their anti-slavery work around a host of domestic responsibilities related both to their families and households and to their husbands' work, though these were of course considerably relieved by the employment of working-class women as servants. Single women like Harriet Martineau who lacked financial support from their families had to restrict their organisational commitments in order to earn their own living through their writing or teaching. Other spinsters, however, like Edinburgh activist Eliza Wigham, were able to devote their lives to good works secure in the financial support of their parents. The time-consuming job of society secretary tended to be filled by single women like Eliza, whereas married women, probably because of their experience with household accounts, tended to be appointed as treasurers.

Many women, both married and single, were — like their menfolk — involved in a wide range of philanthropic and reforming activities in addition to anti-slavery: poor relief, Bible societies, the Anti-Corn Law League, Sunday schools, support for missions, prison visiting and animal welfare. For some, like prison reformer Elizabeth Fry (1780-1845) and ragged and reform school pioneer Mary Carpenter (1807-77), anti-slavery was secondary to their main interest. For others, particularly at the height of anti-slavery agitation in the 1820s and 1830s, it was their main philanthropic preoccupation.

While little information is available on the ordinary subscribing members of ladies' associations there is evidence that the groups tended to be socially exclusive, rarely gaining aristocratic support on the one hand, and making little effort to recruit working-class women on the other.

The names of titled ladies rarely appear among the lists of ladies' association members. Aristocratic women tended to patronise Anglican societies involved in black education and missionary work rather than movements like anti-slavery which were dominated by middle-class nonconformists. The Stafford House Address of 1853, as a major but isolated anti-slavery initiative by aristocratic women, included a statement about the dangers of immediate emancipation, the presence of which suggests that the ladies were out of touch with the mainstream of British anti-slavery thought, which had been 'immediatist' since 1830-31.

Working-class women also seem to have been largely excluded from formal anti-slavery organisation. Scattered acknowledgements of donations from poor women and servants to ladies' anti-slavery associations only confirm their atypicality, and were in any case anonymous donations rather than membership subscriptions. The associations addressed their propaganda at 'ladies' and stressed their respectability. While annual subscription rates of between five and 12 shillings a year were not exorbitant, no attempt was made to encourage working-class involvement by instituting penny-a- week subscriptions on the lines of Bible societies, for example. Such evidence suggests that local ladies' associations in part functioned as social clubs, binding together women from a circumscribed range of backgrounds as members of the philanthropic middle class. Occasionally, however, middle-class women sympathetic to working-class movements did attempt to involve poorer women: Jane Smeal of Glasgow and her friend Elizabeth Pease of Darlington, both Chartist supporters, set their societies' subscription rate at only 2s 6d and Jane commented in 1836 that 'our subscribers and most efficient members are all in the middling and working classes'.[47]

While anti-slavery organisations were predominantly middle class, the movement was dependent for its success on drawing on a far wider section of the population. Extensive public support was essential to maximise the impact of the slave-produce boycott and of petitioning campaigns, and abolitionists found they were able to draw on a wide bedrock of sympathy for the slave. In the 1790s abolitionists remarked on the support for the sugar boycott among domestic servants, the majority of whom were women, and women were specifically included in a boycott call to Methodists, which was a denomination composed mainly of artisan families.[48] Lydia Hardy (d. 1794), wife of shoemaker and radical leader Thomas Hardy and friend of black abolitionist Olaudah Equiano, wrote in 1792 to her husband from her home village of Chesham in Buckinghamshire asking for information of the debate in Parliament against the slave trade, 'for the people here are as much against it as enny ware and there is more people I think hear that drinks tea without sugar than there is drinks with'. Her letter, which goes on to complain about her illness and worries about paying the rent, also vividly illustrates the practical obstacles to working-class women's participation in politics.[49]

There is further evidence for working women's support of abolition in the 1820s and 1830s. Ladies' anti-slavery associations, recognising the importance of public opinion in the pressure to abolish slavery, conducted door-to-door canvasses in an attempt to enlist women's support for boycotts of slave-grown produce, and in some areas met with considerable support and expressions of sympathy among the poor for the suffering slave.[50] In addition, the massive numbers of women who signed the national female anti-slavery petitions and addresses of 1833, 1838 and 1863 suggests considerable working-class support. Much of this was recruited through chapels, and in 1833 almost all Wesleyan Methodist women signed anti-slavery petitions.[51]

Not surprisingly, though, both economic constraints and class antagonism inhibited cross-class co-operation against slavery. Willingness to forego slave-grown produce was limited by the greater expense of 'free'-grown produce.[52]

Middle-class women's concern with preserving respectability was matched by working-class women's cynicism about the hypocrisy of well-to-do campaigners. In 1840 Elizabeth Fry's daughter wrote in horrified tones of an anti-slavery meeting she had attended at Norwich which had been disrupted by Chartists calling for the rights of English white slaves. She remarked — I also saw some women who excited the men, and whose shrill voices out screamed the roar of the men. I heard they were three well-known Socialist sisters, the vilest of the vile..' She compared the event with scenes during the French Revolution, and expressed the hope that the leaders would be punished severely. [53] The women from whom such middle-class reformers recoiled were both Chartists and the likes of Owenite socialist lecturer and freethinker Emma Martin, who in 1844 spoke out against philanthropic ladies who wept over the sufferings of people in distant countries while ignoring the exploitation of poor women in their own land.[54]

Black women, the primary focus of women's abolitionists' concern, opposed slavery in the most immediate sense, by resisting their own oppression. Only a small number, brought like Mary Prince to Britain as slaves, arriving like Ellen Craft as fugitives from slavery, or coming like Sarah Parker Remond as anti-slavery campaigners, participated directly in the British anti-slavery movement. As representatives in the metropolis of their race, and of enslaved women, they nevertheless had an importance out of proportion to their numbers.[55]

Women active in ladies' anti-slavery associations explained their motivations in largely religious terms: as a response to the biblical call to 'remember those in bonds, as bound with them'. 'Negroes', they stated, were God's creatures like themselves, and slavery was an unChristian denial of their humanity. The slogan 'Am I not a man and a brother?', sometimes modified by women into 'Am I not a woman and a sister?' was a key component of the campaign.[56] Slavery was seen as a sin against God, inviting the horrors of divine retribution to fall not only on the planters but also on British people who condoned the system. Emancipation was thus believed to be not only in the interests of the slave but also as essential to the redemption of both the slave-holder and the British nation.[57]

While men also tended to represent their anti-slavery commitment in religious and moral terms, this approach had differing implications for men and women. For men, stress on religion enabled them to raise the cause above the level of party political allegiance. For women, whose proper place was considered to be in the private, domestic sphere, it provided a justification of involvement in public activities generally designated as the province of men. In addition, strong personal religious beliefs gave women the psychological strength to speak out in public against slavery, and even to oppose policies of the male antislavery leadership which they believed to be wrong. Here the concept of religious duty was all-important, a potent combination of Quaker belief in following the 'inner spirit' with the influential evangelical stress on active Christianity and on women's important role as guardians of morality. As the Quaker convert Elizabeth Heyrick asserted: 'truth and justice are stubborn and inflexible, they yield neither to numbers nor authority'.[58] Or as the members of the Sheffield Female Anti-Slavery Society stated in expressing their support for immediate emancipation:

> We ought to obey God rather than man. Confidence here is not at variance with humility. On principles like these, the simple need not fear to comfort the sage; nor a *female* society to take their stand against the united wisdom of this world.[59]

The religious approach to anti-slavery was encouraged by the close links between anti-slavery campaigners and missionaries. As I have already pointed out, ladies' anti-slavery associations made particularly strong connections, frequently allocating a portion of their funds to missionaries involved in black education in the West Indies and Africa. Missionaries in turn wrote to their female supporters about the horrors of slavery, the obstacles it placed in the way of Christianisation, and their own persecution by planters. Some women abolitionists were themselves involved in missionary and educational work. The Quaker Hannah Kilham (1774-1832), for example, set up schools in Sierra Leone to educate black girls rescued from slave ships.[60]

Not all missionaries, however, were opponents of slavery, many being content to condone the system in order to avoid confrontation with the planters, whose supporters themselves frequently quoted the Scriptures in justification of slavery.[61] Tensions between the priorities of missionaries and of abolitionists are apparent in a letter, possibly written by Birmingham campaigner Lucy Townsend, which appeared in the

*Christian Observer,* an Evangelical Anglican magazine. This criticised women like the members of the Ladies' Negro Education Society in London for giving priority to the education of slaves over their release from bondage. The letter writer argued that, rather than educate slaves to prepare them for their freedom, women should join the anti-slavery campaign, since freedom was a precondition for successful education.[62]

For women abolitionists slavery was thus a religious issue because it was an unchristian denial of black humanity, a sin inviting divine retribution, and an obstacle to Christian conversion and education. It was woman's duty to campaign for abolition as a matter of individual conscience and because of her role as guardian and influencer of religion and morality.

The motivation which women campaigners stressed as most specific to and characteristic of their sex was concern for enslaved women. While male campaigners also deplored the sufferings of women and the disruption of family life under slavery, it was women who made this concern the focus of their work, and they who kept the issue before the male leadership .

The first report of the Birmingham Ladies' Society for the Relief of Negro Slaves had on its title page an engraving of a kneeling and enchained woman, with quotes concerning the manacling and flogging of female slaves. Describing the society's formation, its founders Mary Lloyd and Lucy Townsend reported:

> A few individuals who commiserated with the unhappy condition of British negro slaves, and wished to 'remember those in bonds, as bound with them', and who particularly felt for the degraded condition of their own sex, ranked as they are, in the West-India colonies, with the beasts of the field determined to endeavour to awaken (at least in the bosom of English *women*) a deep and lasting compassion, not only for the *bodily suffering* of Female Slaves, but also for their *moral degradation....*[63]

The women had pledged to continue their exertions:

> till the time may come when the lash may no longer be permitted to fall on the persons of helpless Female slaves, ... and when every Negro Mother, living under British Laws, shall press a free-born infant to her bosom.[64]

Similarly, the national female petition of 1833 stated that women were motivated by 'a painful and indignant sense of the injuries offered to their own sex'.[65] Outrage at the physical punishment of women, expressions of horror at their 'humiliation', 'shame' and 'degradation' — the most direct references to sexual abuse and exploitation that middle-class women felt able to make — and opposition to the splitting of families under slavery are all matters which recur again and again in female condemnations of slavery, whether in the form of reports, pamphlets, verses, petitions, addresses or engravings. The Birmingham society commissioned a series of engravings by a local artist to illustrate women's sufferings and placed them in their anti-slavery albums accompanied by appropriate lines of verse. A district treasurer of the Birmingham society, Mrs Phelan, who wrote poetry under the pen-name of Charlotte Elizabeth, composed verses 'On the Flogging of Women', which appealed to male planters thus:

> Bear'st thou a man's, a Christian's name?
> If not for pity, yet for shame,
> Oh fling the scourge wide;
> The tender form may writhe and bleed,
> But deeper cuts thy barbarous deed
> The female's modest pride. [66]

Another woman activist, Elizabeth Heyrick's friend, the teacher and poet Susannah Watts, composed 'The Slave's Address to British Ladies' which contrasted their lot with that of slave women:

> Think, how naught but death can sever
> Your lov'd children from your hold;
> Still alive — but lost forever
> Ours are parted, bought and sold![67]

What was it that made women particularly concerned about the sufferings of their own sex? In the first place this concern was in accord with the general philanthropic preoccupation of middle class women of the period with domestic issues and with the 'oppressed, degraded and heathen' of their own sex. [68] There was a widely held conviction that, as the author of *A Vindication of Female Anti-Slavery Associations* put it: 'pity for suffering, and a desire to relieve misery' are 'the natural and allowed feelings of women'.[69] Allied to this was the belief that women had a special empathy for their own sex: thus the Anti-Slavery Society's 1828 appeal to women described abolition as 'particularly worthy of the female sex' because 'the cruelly degrading and demoralising effects of slavery on the female character are so strongly marked'.[70] The focus on enslaved women probably also resulted from the desire of British women to delineate a specific field of expertise for the separate ladies' anti-slavery associations they formed from 1825 onwards.

For a variety of reasons women in Britain thus came to believe that it was their moral and religious duty to speak on behalf of enslaved women in the Caribbean and elsewhere. These women were represented as passive victims, as 'the weakest and most succourless of the human race'.[71] It was British women's duty 'to plead for those of their own sex, who have less power to plead than ourselves, who cannot speak their Misery and their shame'.[72]

It is important to question whether this representation of women slaves accurately reflected black women's experiences. Enslaved women did suffer from particular and terrible forms of oppression because of their sex: they were forced to do heavy manual labour when pregnant and nursing, they were subject to sexual degradation through being stripped for flogging by male overseers, they were raped and sexually exploited by their masters, and their infants were torn from them for sale to other owners. It is clear, however, that women slaves were not the mute, passive and degraded victims which female abolitionists made them out to be. They cultivated crops on their small provision grounds and sold surpluses, or they took in laundry, trying to amass enough money to buy their own or their children's freedom. They spoke out against unjust punishments, and even appealed to the courts for redress. They gave support to, and made sacrifices for, each other. They undermined the system through working slowly or badly. Most dramatically, they ran away from their owners, sabotaged plantations, poisoned their owners or joined slave rebellions.[73] The lives of individuals like Mary Prince and Ellen Craft, who are exceptional only in the opportunity they had to write and speak against slavery in Britain, exemplify both the victimisation of women under slavery and their resistance and survival.

Why, then, did white women represent black women as passive victims rather than recognising their strategies for survival and histories of resistance? A number of reasons can be suggested. Firstly, the image of passive female suffering was tactically useful: it was likely to arouse pity in middle-class women schooled in the virtues of suffering without complaint, and in the Quaker pacifists who were so prominent in the anti-slavery movement.

The victim stereotype, with its accompanying stress on black women's natural modesty and desire for family life, can also be interpreted as an attempt by white women to counteract the stories of rampant black female sexuality put about by apologists of slavery. In a complementary way, women campaigners counterposed the planter's spectre of the murderous, rapacious male slave who was a threat to white womanhood with an image of black men denied 'the authority and rights of husbands' over their womenfolk and who were thus unable 'to protect them from insult'.[74] Elizabeth Heyrick explained the slave revolt in Demerara in 1823 as the response of men to being forcibly separated from their families and witnessing their wives being compelled to become the mistresses of overseers.[75]

Criticism of the disruption of family life and the degradation of women under slavery was linked to women campaigners' vision of the ideal post-emancipation society in the West Indies. It was a vision rooted in a dominant middle-class ideology which encompassed gender as well as race and class. In terms of class, post-emancipation society should be based on the substitution of slave labour by 'free' — i.e. waged — labour. In racial terms, it should be a society in which control passed from white planters corrupted by slavery, to a benevolent colonial empire bringing the light of western civilisation, legitimate commerce and Christian education of the 'benighted races'. In terms of gender, it should be an arena in which the sexual exploitation of women and the disruption of family life was replaced by a society in which the black woman was able 'to occupy her proper Station as a Daughter, a Wife, and a Mother'.[76] For, as women had stated in the 1825 'Appeal from British Ladies to the West India Planters':

> it has wounded us to read of woman's suffering and woman's humiliation in Countries which acknowledge British laws, which are governed, not by some half-wild, benighted Race, but by those who are connected with us by the closest ties.[77]

Middle-class white women's condemnation of slavery and their vision of freedom were tied to their ideas about British society. David Brion Davis has convincingly linked the anti-slavery leadership's contrasting of slave labour with 'free' labour to industrial capitalists' desire to maintain control over their employees by obscuring the exploitation involved in waged labour.[78] In a parallel way, the contrast made between the 'hapless and forlorn 'lot of enslaved women' and the 'high privileges as British females' can be linked to the desire of middle-class campaigners to regulate working-class family life and to deny the oppression of working-class women as the lowest-paid workers.[79]

For the *women* campaigners who used this campaigning language, however, there were oppressive implications for their *own* lives as white, middle-class women as well as for the lives of other women, black and working-class. For behind the rhetoric of female privilege and male protection lay the reality that in early nineteenth-century Britain married women lacked any independent legal rights, making them defenceless against domestic violence and sexual abuse, and giving their husbands total control of their children and their property.[80] In this context, the 'proper station' which white women called for on behalf of black women — and indeed themselves — was one subordinate to their menfolk. At a men's reception to celebrate the emancipation of slaves, held after the wedding of anti-slavery activist Priscilla Buxton, the bride was toasted with the wish 'that she might long rejoice in the fetters put on that day as well as over those which she had assisted to break'.[81]

In the British anti-slavery movement, women's concern for other women was thus based on a limited vision of liberty. What then was the relationship between anti-slavery and the development of feminism, a movement which shared with anti-slavery an articulation of female oppression, and which also organised women to campaign against female subordination and to obtain rights?[82]

While British women were campaigning on behalf of their enslaved sisters in the West Indies and the United States, a movement was developing for the rights of women within Britain itself. The anti-slavery movement spanned the period between Mary Wollstonecraft's key feminist work, *A Vindication of the Rights of Women* (1792) and the formation of the first women's suffrage societies in 1867. The origins of modern feminism thus lay in the period of anti-slavery organisation.[83]

The personnel involved in the two movements overlapped. Among women who were both leading anti-slavery activists and supporters of women's rights were Anne Knight and Harriet Martineau (from the 1830s), Elizabeth Pease (from the 1840s), Harriet Lupton and Rebecca Moore (from the 1850s).[84] From the 1840s the Unitarian educationalist Elizabeth Jessup Reid (1787-1866) combined support for anti-slavery with campaigning for higher education for women and married women's property rights. Sarah Parker Remond, who boarded with Elizabeth Reid and was her student at Bedford College in London, provided a personal transatlantic link between women involved in both abolitionist and feminist movements. She had attended women's rights conventions in the United States before coming to Britain in 1859 and becoming the first female anti-slavery lecturer.[85]

For British women anti-slavery campaigners, their feminism grew out of their own experiences within Britain and also in response to the stimulus of the American abolitionist-feminists with whom they were in close contact.[86] In contrast to their American sisters, however, British women were cautious about raising the issue of women's rights within the British anti-slavery movement and, as we have seen, it was not until the 1850s that a few tentative steps were made in this direction.

What is more striking is the number of leading female anti-slavery activists of the 1840-1868 period who went on to become leaders of campaigns for women's rights from the late 1860s onwards. Harriet Martineau, Mary Estlin, Elizabeth Pease and Eliza Wigham and other anti-slavery activists became leaders of the feminist campaign of 1869-1886 for the repeal of the Contagious Diseases Acts. As Judy Walkowitz has pointed out, the members of this new campaign referred to themselves as abolitionists and adopted the language of anti-slavery. Josephine Butler (1828-1906), who led the crusade, described the Contagious Diseases Acts as a 'legislative movement for the creation of a slave class of women for the supposed benefit of licentious men.[87]

Many of this same core group of women abolitionists also took leading roles in the women's suffrage movement, in promoting higher education for women, and in campaigning for a married women's property act. In addition, a new group of women's rights campaigners, mainly Liberals in political affiliation, joined in the final stages of the anti-slavery campaign in the 1860s; Priscilla Bright Maclaren, who joined Eliza Wigham on the committee of the Edinburgh Ladies' Emancipation Society and as a co-leader of the women's suffrage; Clementia Taylor, who founded both the Ladies' London Emancipation Society and the London National Society for Women's Suffrage; Emily Faithfull of the Victoria Press, who published both the first British feminist magazine, the *English Woman's Journal,* and a series of anti-slavery tracts written and compiled by the Ladies' London Emancipation Society. Among the authors of these tracts were Frances Power Cobbe, another leader of the women's suffrage movement, and Emily Shirreff, a pioneer in women's education.[88]

Despite evidence for the overlap in leading personnel between anti-slavery and feminism, the passage from support for abolition to support for women's rights was fraught with obstacles, and many women active in the anti-slavery movement never became feminists.

These barriers to the development of a feminist consciousness were related in the way in which women conceptualised and justified their anti-slavery activities. Women activists in general did not directly challenge the ideology of 'separate spheres', representing their work as moral and religious rather than political, and their petitioning as an exceptional response to exceptional circumstances rather than as a precedent for fuller political participation by women. They couched their anti-slavery commitment in the language of duties rather than the language of rights. Ann Taylor Gilbert (1782-1866), an evangelical hymn-writer married to an Independent minister, organised the massive Nottingham women's petition against slavery in 1833 and stated that she had 'no scruple, as to female petitions, in the case of humanity'. However, when asked by Anne Knight to lend her support to a campaign for women's rights, she replied that she was not in favour of women having the vote. She considered that women were adequately represented by their menfolk and that the 'division of labour' and of 'spheres' was both the natural and scientific way to organise society, which avoided creating conflict within the family and burdening women with extra responsibilities on top of their heavy load of domestic and philanthropic duties.[89]

There was also a tension between the discourses of anti-slavery and of feminism, stemming from their different objectives. As we have seen, middle-class women campaigners *contrasted* their own privileged lot with that of enslaved women. On the other hand, supporters of women's rights *compared* the position of women and slaves.

This woman/slave analogy tended to surface at high points in the popular anti-slavery campaigns: in the work of Mary Wollstonecraft in the 1790s and in the statements of Owenite socialists such as William Thompson, Anna Wheeler and working-class lecturers Eliza Macaulay and Frances Morrison in the 1820s and 1830s.[90] It also occurs in the writings of feminists who were anti-slavery activists: in Harriet Martineau's *Society in America* (1837); in Marion Reid's *A Plea for Woman* (1843), the work of a Scotswoman who had attended the World Anti-Slavery Convention in London in 1840.[91]

It is probably significant, however, that both the latter works were written after the passage of the 1833 Emancipation Act. For the woman/

slave analogy posed a danger to the anti-slavery campaign in its tendency to make invisible the particular oppression of black women, both on account of their gender and because of their race. There were comparable problems with the working-class slave analogy used by Chartist men and women, since this obscured the oppression of slaves both as workers and as unwaged chattels. This is not of course to deny that both analogies drew their strength from real experiences and feelings of oppression, in addition to being powerful rhetorical devices.

Black women themselves attempted to combat the tendency of such analogies to obscure the greater oppression suffered by enslaved women in comparison to poor white women. Ellen Craft, in response to rumours that she was disillusioned with her life of freedom in Britain, wrote in 1852 to the editor of the *Anti-Slavery Advocate*: 'I had much rather starve in England, a free woman, than be a slave for the best man that ever breathed upon the American continent.[92] Sarah Parker Remond stated that:

> she knew something of the trials and toils of the women of England — how ... they were made to 'Stitch, stitch, stitch,' till weariness and exhaustion overtook them. But there was this immeasurable difference between their condition and that of the slave-woman, that their persons were free and their progeny their own, while the slavewoman was the victim of the heartless lust of her master, and the children whom she bore were his property.[93]

If the woman-worker/slave analogy obscured the particular oppression suffered by black women slaves, the rhetoric of sisterhood used by female anti-slavery campaigners raises rather different problems. It is clear that the term 'sister' meant different things when applied to different women. Thus the slogan 'Am I not a woman and a sister' was used by white women to emphasise the essential humanity of enslaved women, and the sympathy which women felt for their own sex, but it was not intended as an assertion of cultural equality. Only the small number of black women who, like Sarah Remond, were Western educated and Christian, were admitted into the sisterhood of Anglo-American reformers as cultural equals.

In this context there are interesting parallels between middle-class women's approaches to anti-slavery and to the campaign against the Contagious Diseases Acts: both were based on ideals of sisterhood, but both tended to treat the women on whose behalf they campaigned black women slaves and English working-class prostitutes respectively — as helpless victims. In contrast, the ideal of Anglo-Saxon sisterhood evoked by white British and American women anti-slavery campaigners stressed racial and cultural identification across national boundaries. It tended to render invisible black women's contributions to the Anglo-American anti-slavery movement, and implicitly evoked an ideal of white racial solidarity as the basis for sisterhood.

White middle-class women's conceptions of liberty and equality were thus specific in terms of both race and class. Within the anti-slavery campaign, their own empowerment as women was based on the disempowerment of black women, whose characterisation as silent victims provided the justification for women campaigners to speak out on their behalf, to move into the public and political arena, and to organise together in sisterly networks. But there was also an opposite side to the coin: emancipation from slavery was a form of empowerment sought and fought for by black women themselves, white middle-class women's insistence on their own privileged position as women in British society was disempowering to themselves in inhibiting the development of feminism.

White women anti-slavery campaigners in 19th century Britain are the foremothers of white women involved in anti-racist work today. As I have tried to show, however, they provide ambivalent role models. On the positive side, we can gain inspiration from individual women like Elizabeth Heyrick, who defied male authority and followed the dictates of her own conscience in calling publicly for immediate emancipation, and from the tens of thousands of women who broke with social convention to petition Parliament for the end of slavery. The particular strengths of women in organising at a local community level on issues like the consumer boycott also provide an example to present-day campaigners. As feminists, the strengths of women-only organisations are confirmed, and the concern women expressed for the particular sufferings of their own sex accords with our political perspective today.

On the other hand, our foremothers' organisations, actions and ideologies need to be viewed critically from several perspectives: the class-based exclusivity of ladies' anti-slavery associations; the cultural baggage of deeply held beliefs in western and Christian superiority which led white women to promote imperialism while campaigning against slavery; and the tendency to represent the enslaved women on whose behalf they campaigned as passive victims.

The legacy of both the strengths and the limitations in the vision of our foremothers has been bequeathed to the British feminist movement today. This legacy must be acknowledged and confronted if there is to be a basis for true sisterhood between all women. The empowerment of women will have to be founded on knowledge of our different but intersecting histories, and of the changing ways in which dominant politics of gender have interacted with those of race and class to separate and disempower us.

## Notes

1. This biblical quotation appears at the opening of the *First Report of the Female Society. for Birmingham. West-Bromwich. Wednesbury, Walsall. and Their Respective Neighbourhoods, for the Relief of British Negro Slaves*, (Birmingham: B. Hudson, 1826), p. 3.

2. For publications which have begun the process of recovering these histories: Barbara Bush, *Slave Women in Caribbean society, 1650-1832*, (Bloomington: Indiana University Press, 1989); and a valuable article by Louis and Rosamund Billington, 'A Burning Zeal for Righteousness': Women in the British Anti-Slavery Movement, 1820-1860', in Jane Rendall, ed., *Equal or Different: Women's Politics 1800-1914*, (Blackwell, 1987), PP. 82-111.

3. I would like to acknowledge the helpful comments on this essay which I received from Joan Grant and from members of the London Feminist History Group. For a fuller account of women campaigners see Clare Midgley, *Women Against Slavery: the British Campaigns, 1780-1870* (London: Routledge, 1992)

4. By both 'race' and 'gender' I mean socially constructed categories and hierarchies rather than biological, 'natural' ones.

5. See for example Hazel V. Carby, 'White Woman Listen! Black Feminism and the Boundaries of Sisterhood', Centre for Contemporary Cultural Studies, *The Empire Strikes Back: Race and Racism in 70s Britain* (London: Hutchinson, 1982); Valerie Amos and Pratibha Parmar, 'Challenging Imperial Feminism', *Feminist Review*, no. 17, (July 1984), pp. 3-19.

6. For further information on slavery within Britain and on Granville Sharpe's efforts to establish its illegality see F.O. Shyllon, *Black Slaves in Britain* (London: Oxford University Press, 1974); Peter Fryer, *Staying Power: The History of Black People in Britain* (London: Pluto Press, 1984).

7. Susanne Everett, *The Slaves*, (London: Bison Books), p. 36. See also Philip D. Curtin, *The Atlantic Slave Trade. A Census* (London: Macmillan, 1965).

8. For a discussion of Lady Middleton's influence on William Wilberforce see John Pollock, *Wilberforce*, (Tring: Lion, 1978), p. 53.

9. *List of the Society. Instituted in 1787 for the Purpose of Effecting the Abolition of the Slave Trade*, (London, 1788); letter from 'C' printed in the *Manchester Mercury*, 6th November 1787.

10. Mary Birkett, *A Poem on the African Slave Trade. Addressed to Her Own Sex*, (Dublin: J. Jones, 1792), Part I, verse 26, line 13.

11. Thomas Clarkson, *The History of the Rise. Progress. and Accomplishment of the Abolition of the African Slave-Trade by the British Parliament,* 2 Vols., (London: Longman, Hirst, Rees and Orme, 1808), Vol. II, p. 350.

12. Women comprise a quarter of the British authors of imaginative anti-slavery literature listed in Peter Hogg's *The African Slave Trade and its Suppression: Classified and Annotated Bibliography* (London: Frank Cass, 1973).

13. 'On the Slave Trade by a Young Lady at School', poem printed in the *Manchester Mercury,* 4 March 1788; Hannah More, *Slavery, a Poem,* (London: T. Cadell, 1788); William Roberts (ed.), *Memoirs of the Life and Correspondence of Mrs Hannah More*, (2nd ed., 4 Vols., London: R.B. Seeley and W. Burnside, 1834), Vol. II, p. 97.

14. *Manchester Mercury,* 4 December 1789.

15. Mary Wollstonecraft, *A Vindication of the rights of Women* (2nd ed., London: J. Johnson, 1790). pp. 24, 128, 129-30; Helen Maria Williams, *Letters on the French Revolution*, (1st American ed., Boston: J. Belknap and A. Young, 1791), p. 33; report of petition from the inhabitants of Belford in Northumberland, *Newcastle Courant,* 3 March 1792; reports of debates in *Morning Herald,* 27 Feb 1788, *Morning Chronicle*, 7 Apr 1788.

16. For a general account of slavery in the British colonies see Michael Craton, *Sinews of Empire, a Short History of British Slavery* (London, 1974).

17. A decision to promote ladies' associations was taken at a meeting of the national committee on 11th May 1825, after it had been informed of the foundation of a women's society in Birmingham (see Committee on Slavery Minute Book, entry for 11th May 1825, among Anti-Slavery Papers, Rhodes House Library, Oxford). For Wilberforce's objections see Robert Isaac and Samuel Wilberforce, *The Life of William Wilberforce,* 5 Vols., (London: John Murray, 1840), Vol. V, p. 264, quotation from letter dated 31 January 1826.

18. *Account of the Receipts and Disbursements of the Anti-Slavery Society. for the Year 1831: with a List of Subscribers* (London: Bagster and Thoms). This list represents only those groups sending money to the national society in that year. I have identified a total of 73 ladies' associations active at some time between 1825 and 1833.

19. Frank Prochaska, *Women and Philanthropy in Nineteenth Century England,* (Oxford: Oxford University Press, 1980), pp. 22-29.

20. *The First, Second. Third and Fifth Reports of the Female Society for Birmingham, West Bromwich. Wednesbury. and their Respective Neighbourhoods. for the Relief of British Negro Slaves*, (Birmingham: B. Hudson, 1826-1828, 1830); minute book, cash book, album and ledger of the Ladies' Society for the Relief of Negro Slaves, for Birmingham etc, in Birmingham Central Library, Archives Dept. (note: the name of the society varied slightly over time). For income compare accounts at the end of *First Report of the Female Society, for Birmingham* with *Account of the Receipts and Disbursements of the Anti-Slavery Society for the Years 1823, 1824, 1826 and 1828* (London), p. 8.

21. *Account of the Receipts and Disbursements of the Anti-Slavery Society for the Years 1829 and 1830,* (London), pp. 6-10 .

22. See for example *Third Report of the Female Society for Birmingham,* p. 17; *Report of the Sheffield Female Anti-Slavery Society*, (Sheffield, 1827), p. 3.

23. *The History of Mary Prince*, ed. Moira Ferguson, (London: Pandora, 1987 reprint of the original 1831 edition, with a new introduction), pp. 64, 84.

24. [Elizabeth Heyrick], *Immediate. not Gradual Abolition: or an Enquiry into the Shortest Safest and Most Effectual Means of Getting Rid of West Indian Slavery*, (London, 1824), p. 18. For a full list of Heyrick's pamphlets on slavery and other issues and a valuable, though in my opinion over-cautious, assessment of Heyrick's influence on anti-slavery policy, see Kenneth Corfield, 'Elizabeth Heyrick: Radical Quaker', in Gail Malmgreen, ed., *Religion in the Lives of English Women, 1760-1830* (London; Croom Helm, 1986), pp. 41-67.

25. Minute Book of the Ladies' Society for the Relief of Negro Slaves, entry for 8th April 1830; *Report of the Agency Committee of the Anti-Slavery Society,* (London: S. Bagster Jun., 1832).

26. For information on petitions see *Journals of the House of Commons,* Vols. 86 to 88 (1830-1833); *Journals of the House of Lords,* Vols. 62 to 65 (1830-33); *First to Forty-First Reports of the Select Committee on Public Petitions* (1833).

27. Sir George Stephen, *Anti-Slavery Recollections: in a Series of Letters. Addressed to Mrs Beecher Stowe,* (London: Thomas Hatchard, 1854), pp. 196-7; *Record,* 16th May 1833; *Anti-Slavery Advocate,* Vol. IV, no. 175 (6th May 1833), p. 140; London Female Anti-Slavery Society, 'Female Petition for the Abolition of Slavery' (printed circular issued 29th April 1833); 'The Ladies of the London Female Anti-Slavery Society ...' (printed circular issued London, May 1833).

28. See for example *Eleventh Report of the Ladies' Negro's Friend Society. for Birmingham,* (Birmingham: B. Hudson, 1836).

29. For report of Exeter Hall meeting see *Christian Advocate,* Vol. VIII, no. 394 (July 1837), p. 225; for text of addresses and numbers of signatories see Ibid., Vol. IX, no. 425 (19 Feb 1838), pp. 56, 63; Ibid., Vol IX, no 439 (28 May 1838), p.171; *British Emancipator,* no. 8 (21 Mar 1838), p. 43.

30. *The British Emancipator,* No. VII (March 14, 1838), p. 36.

31. Many of the Reports of the Edinburgh Ladies' Emancipation Society are in the National Library of Scotland; the minute books of the Bristol and Clifton Ladies' Anti-Slavery Society are among the Estlin Papers in Dr Williams Library, London.

32. See Donald R. Kennon, ''An Apple of Discord': The Woman Question at the World's Anti-Slavery Convention of 1840', *Slavery and Abolition,* vol. V, no. 3 (Dec 1984), pp. 244-266.

33. *Fifth to Twentieth Annual Reports of the British and Foreign Anti-Slavery Society* (London: Johnston and Barrett, 1844-1859).

34. For the free produce movement see *The Slave* (a periodical which Anna Richardson edited in 1851-55); for bazaars see notices in the *British and Foreign Anti-Slavery Reporter* from 1845 and in the *Anti-Slavery Advocate* from 1853; for the text of the Stafford House Address see the London *Times* 29 November 1852, p.8.

35. William and Ellen Craft, *Running a Thousand Miles for Freedom,* (London: William Tweedie, 1860); R.J.M. Blackett, 'Fugitive Slaves in Britain: the Odyssey of William and Ellen Craft', *Journal of American Studies,* Vol. XII (1978), pp. 41-61.

36. There is a considerable amount of scattered information on Julia Griffiths in Philip S. Foner, *Frederick Douglass: a Biography* (New York: Citadel Press, 1966); information on the societies she formed in Britain is contained in issues of the *British and Foreign Anti-Slavery Reporter* for 1856 and 1857.

37. An enormous collection of this transatlantic correspondence is preserved in the Anti-Slavery Collection in Boston Public Library, Massachusetts. A selection is

printed in Clare Taylor, ed., *British and American Abolitionists*, (Edinburgh University Press, 1974).

38. *First Annual Report of the Leeds Anti-slavery Association*, (Leeds: W. Walker, 1854)
39. Letter from Rebecca Moore to R.D. Webb, London, 30th November 1854 (MS A.1.2. v. 26, p. 37 in Anti-Slavery Collection, Boston Public Library); minute book of the Bristol and Clifton Ladies' Anti-Slavery Society (Dr Williams Library), entries for 16th and 24th November 1854.
40. For reports of Remond's lectures see *Anti-Slavery Reporter and Anti-Slavery Advocate*, various dates, February 1859 to February 1861.
41. The minutes of the London Emancipation Committee are among the George Thompson Papers, John Rylands University Library, Manchester.
42. *Daily News*, 30th August 1861, p. 4. For a valuable recent biography of Martineau see Valerie Kossew Pichanick, *Harriet Martineau: the Woman and her Work. 1802-76*, (Ann Arbor: University of Michigan Press, 1980), (p. 213 assesses her *Daily News* articles).
43. *The First and Second Annual Reports of the Ladies' London Emancipation Society*, (London, 1864, 1865).
44. Alex Tyrrell, *Joseph Sturge and the Moral Radical Party in Early Victorian Britain*, (London; Christopher Helm, 1987). See pp. 12, 15, 50,57, 62-3, 80, 130, 139, 156, 184, 208 for references to Sophia.
45. Anna M. Stoddart, *Elizabeth Pease Nichol*, (London: J.M. Dent, 1899).
46. Letter from Mary Ann Estlin to Emma Weston, Park St., Bristol, 21st October 1851 (Ms. A.7.3. p. 33, Anti-Slavery Collection, Boston Public Library).
47. Glasgow Ladies' Auxiliary Emancipation Society, *Three Years' Female Anti-Slavery Effort. in Britain and America* (Glasgow: Aird and Russell, 1837), pp. 65-71; *Darlington Ladies Society for The Universal Abolition of Slavery* [Rules and Report, ca 1837]; letter from Jane Smeal to Elizabeth Pease, Glasgow, 21 Dec 1836, printed in Taylor, ed., *British and American Abolitionists*, p. 54.
48. Thomas Clarkson, *The History of the Rise*, Vol. II, p. 349; Samuel Bradburn, *An Address to the People Called Methodists; Concerning the Evil of Encouraging the Slave Trade*, (Manchester: T. Harper), pp. 12-18.
49. Letter from Lydia Hardy to Thomas Hardy, Chesham, 2 April 1792, Public Record Office, Chancery Lane, London (ref: TS 24/12/1).
50. See for example *Report of the Sheffield Female Anti-Slavery Society*, (Sheffield, 1827), p. 3.
51. It has been estimated that 95.2 % of Wesleyan Methodist — 229,426 men and women out of a denominational membership of around 241,000 — signed anti-slavery petitions in 1833 (see Seymour Drescher, 'Two Variables of Anti-Slavery: Religious Organisation and Social Mobilisation in Britain and France, 1780- 1870', in Christine Bolt and Seymour Drescher, eds., *Anti-Slavery, Religion and Reform*, (Folkestone: Dawson, 1980), chap. II, table 2.
52. Problems encountered in Wiltshire in the 1820s are discussed in the Minute Book of the Ladies' Society for the Relief of Negro Slaves (Birmingham Central Reference Library), entry for 26th November 1829.
53. Letter from Katherine Fry to Mrs Louisa Pelly, Earlham, Nov 19, 1840, Buxton Papers, Vol. 20, pp. 37-43, Mss. Brit. Emp. S. 444, Anti-Slavery Papers, Rhodes House Library, Oxford.

54. Emma Martin, *The Missionary Jubilee Panic* (1844), p. 3, as quoted in Barbara Taylor, *Eve and the New Jerusalem*, p. 152.

55. C. Peter Ripley, *The Black Abolitionist Papers*, Vol I: The British Isles, 1830-1865, (Chapel Hill: University of North Carolina Press, [ca. 1985] lists nine black abolitionist women in Britain at this period: Clarissa Brown, Josephine Brown, Harriet Brent Jacobs, 'Josephine', Caroline Putman, Frances Russell and Mary E. Webb in addition to Ellen Craft and Sarah Parker Remond.

56. While the Wedgwood seal of an enslaved man with the motto 'Am I not a man and a brother' was first produced in 1787, the earliest use of a parallel image of an enslaved woman occurred in 1826 at the head of the *First Report of the Female Society for Birmingham*, and by 1828 this society was producing seals bearing the motto 'Am I not a woman and a sister' (the seals listed in the *Rules and Resolutions of the Dublin Ladies' Anti-Slavery Society* (Dublin: printed for the Society, 1828), p. 16 were supplied by the Birmingham women (see the *Third Report of the Female Society for Birmingham*, p. 54).

57. Elizabeth Heyrick, *Immediate, not Gradual Abolition*, p.7

58. *Ibid*

59. *Report of the Sheffield Female Anti-Slavery Society*, (Sheffield, 1827), p. 10.

60. Mora Dickson, *The Powerful Bond: Hannah Kilham 1774-1832*, (London: Dennis Dobson, 1980).

61. Mary Turner, *Slaves and Missionaries: the Disintegration of Jamaican Slave Society. 1787-1834*, (Urbana: University of Illinois Press, 1982).

62. Letter from 'BTWL', *Christian Observer*, Vol. XXV no 12 (Dec 1825), pp. 749-51, a modified version of which is copied into Lucy Townsend's Scrap Book on Negro Slaves, pp. 151-5 (Mss Brit. Emp. S 4, Anti-Slavery Papers, Rhodes House Library, Oxford).

63. *The First Report of the Female Society, for Birmingham. West- Bromwich, Wednesbury. Walsall. and their Respective Neighbourhoods. for the Relief of British Negro Slaves*, (Birmingham, 1826), p. 3.

64. *Ladies Society for the Relief of Negro Slaves. Founding Meeting held West-Bromwich*, 8th April 1825. Eighth resolution.

65. For the full text of the national petition see *Twentieth Report of the Select Committee on Public Petitions* (London: House of Commons, 1833), Appendix no. 701.

66. This poem was included in the Album of the Female Society for Birmingham (in Birmingham Central Reference Library).

67. This poem was printed at the head of *The Third Report of the Female Society for Birmingham* (Birmingham, 1828).

68. See Frank Prochaska, *Women and Philanthropy in Nineteenth Century England*, (Oxford University Press, 1980), especially p. 30.

69. *A Vindication of Female Anti-Slavery Associations*, (London: printed for the Female Anti-Slavery Society, [n.d.]), p. 3.

70. *A Picture of Colonial Slavery. in the Year 1828. Addressed Especially to the Ladies of Great Britain*, [London: Anti-Slavery Society, 1828], pp. 5-6.

71. *The Second Annual Report of the Ladies' Association for Calne*, (Calne: W. Baily, 1827), p. 4.

72. 'Appeal from British Ladies to the West India Planters' (1825), Lucy Townsend's Scrap Book on Negro Slaves (Rhodes House Library) p. 127.

73. The information given here on the lives, oppression and resistance of enslaved women is taken from Rhoda E. Reddock, 'Women and Slavery in the Caribbean: A Feminist Perspective', *Latin American Perspectives*, Issue 44, Vol. XII, no. 1 (Winter 1985), pp. 63-80, and from the following articles by Barbara Bush: 'Defiance or Submission? The Role of the Slave Woman in Slave Resistance in the British Caribbean'. *Immigrants and Minorities*, Vol. 1, no. 1 (1982), pp. 16-38; ''The Family Tree ~ Not Cut': Women and Cultural Resistance in Slave Family Life in the British Caribbean', G. Okihiro, ed., *In Resistance: Studies in African. Caribbean and Afro-American history,* (Amherst: Massachusetts University Press, 1986), pp. 117-132; 'Towards Emancipation: Slave Women and Resistance to Coercive Labour Regimes in the British West Indian Colonies, 1790-1838', *Slavery and Abolition,* Vol V, no. 3 (Dec 1984), pp. 222-243.

74. 'Appeal from British Ladies to the West India Planters', Lucy Townsend's Scrap Book on Negro Slaves (Rhodes House Library). P.134

75. Elizabeth Heyrick], *Immediate, not Gradual Abolition*, p.22.

76. Quote from petition of the women of Spilsby in Lincolnshire to the House of Lords, 28th March 1833 (see *Journal of the House of Lords*, (London), session 1833, Vol. LXV, p. 121).

77. Lucy Townsend's Scrap Book on Negro Slaves (Rhodes House Library), p. 127.

78. Davis employs Antonio Gramsci's concept of ideological hegemony to describe this process (see D.B. Davis, *The Problem of Slavery in the Age of Revolution*, (Ithaca: Cornell University Press, 1975)).

79. See Birmingham women's 1830 Address to the Queen in the Minute Book of the Ladies Society for the Relief of Negro Slaves (Birmingham Central Reference Library), entry for 23rd December 1830; 1833 petition from the ladies of Market Lavington to the House of Commons in *Nineteenth Report from the Select Committee on Public Petitions* (London: House of Commons), Appendix no. 675.

80. For information on women's legal status in nineteenth century Britain see Ray Strachey, *The Cause. A Short History of the Women's Movement in Great Britain*, (London: Virago, 1978 reprint of 1938 original edition).

81. Extract from the journal of Anna Gurney and Sarah Buxton, Buxton Papers, Vol. XII, pp. 111-113, MSS Brit. Emp. S.444, Rhodes House Library.

82. For a further dimension on these issues see Clare Midgley, 'Anti-Slavery and Feminism in Nineteenth Century Britain', *Gender and History* Vol.5 No.3 (Autumn 1993) pp.343-362.

83. See Jane Rendall, *The Origins of Modern Feminism: Women in Britain, France and the United States, 1780-1860*, (Basingstoke: Macmillan, 1985).

84. For information on Anne Knight (1786-1862), an outspoken Quaker radical from Chelmsford in Essex who had close contacts with French socialists and feminists, see Gail Malmgreen, 'Anne Knight and the Radical Subculture', *Quaker History,* Vol. LXXI, no. 2 (Fall 1982), pp. 100-113.

85. Ruth Bogin, 'Sarah Parker Remond: Black Abolitionist from Salem', *Essex Institute Historical Collections*, Vol. CX (April 1974), pp. 120-150; Dorothy B. Porter, 'Sarah Parker Remond, Abolitionist and Physician', *Journal of Negro History*, Vol. XX, no. 3 (July 1935), pp. 287-293.

86. For information of women abolitionists in the United States see Blanche Glassman Hersch, *The Slavery of Sex. Feminist- Abolitionists in America,* (Urbana: University

of Illinois Press, 1978); Alma Lutz, *Crusade for Freedom: Women of the Anti-slavery Movement,* (Boston: Beacon Press, 1968).

87. Judith R. Walkowitz, *Prostitution and Victorian Society Women, Class. and the State* (Cambridge University Press, 1980). Walkowitz identifies 10 of the 33 members of the female leadership as involved in anti-slavery (see Table I, pp. 126-7). The quotation is from Josephine E. Butler, *Personal Reminiscences of a Great Crusade,* (London: Horace Marshall, 1986), p. 81.

88. *The First and Second Annual Reports of the Ladies' London Emancipation Society,* (London, 1864, 1865). For information on the Liberal feminist group see Jane Rendall, ''A Moral Engine'? Feminism, Liberalism and the *English Woman's Journal'*, Rendall, ed., *Equal or Different,* pp. 112-138.

89. Autobiography and Other Memorials of Mrs Gilbert, (Formerly Ann Taylor), ed. Josiah Gilbert, 2 Vols., (London: Henry S. King and Co, 1874), Vol II, p. 162, pp. 185-188.

90. For Wollstonecraft's references to female slavery see Mary Wollstonecraft, *A Vindication of the Rights of Women,* ed. Carol H. Poston (New York: W.W. Norton and Co., 1975), pp. 35, 37, 61, 167; for information on Owenite socialist feminists and the woman/slave analogy see Barbara Taylor, *Eve and the New Jerusalem* (Virago, 1984), especially pp. 34-35, 96.

91. Harriet Martineau, *Society in America,* 3 Vols. (London: Saunders and Otley, 1837), Vol. I, pp. 201-204, Vol. III, p. 106; Marion Reid, *A Plea for Woman,* (Edinburgh: Polygon, 1988). Anne Knight's annotated copy of the book is preserved in Friends' House Library, London.

92. *Anti-Slavery Advocate,* Vol. I, no. 3 (Dec 1852), p. 22.

93. Speech by Sarah Parker Remond in the Music Hall, Store Street, 15th June 1859, as reported in the *Anti-Slavery Reporter,* 3rd Series, vol. VII, no. 7 (July 1859), p. 150.

# 5

# Some Of Us Are Imperialists, Some Of Us Are Not

*Florence Hamilton*

Traditional descriptions of British women in British India have focused on their missionary, their memsahib and pioneering roles.

The women who feature in this study can be divided into groups according to what they actually did or what their connection was with India: as memsahibs, welfare workers, reforming feminists, international socialists, supporters of liberation movements, political writers and pacifists. Some lived and worked in India and have left records of their involvement in social reform campaigns, the women's movement and nationalist organisations. Others learned about British rule in India through an interest in international affairs and joined British-based groups aiming to improve relations between Britain and India or to build support for Indian nationalism.

## Background to the British in India

In 1618 the British East India Company obtained trading rights from the Mughals. The EIC aimed to buy Indian products as cheaply as possible for resale at high prices in European markets. Although the Indian economy was running productively, the disintegration of Mughal influence and subsequent political conflict created a power vacuum which the EIC exploited to their own advantage.

After 1757 the EIC took military control in Bengal. Its methods of operation were criticised in Britain as well as in India, and as industrial development progressed in England, Bengal's agriculture and commerce declined under the pressure of EIC activities. The accumulated wealth known as the 'Bengal plunder' boosted British industrialisation: from 1760 the flying shuttle, the spinning jenny, the power loom and the steam engine were set in motion. Lancashire businessmen demanded a 'free market' for cotton goods to be imported into India. In 1813 the EIC monopoly of Indian trade ended, and India became a major market for cotton, silk, wool, paper and glass. British legislation made direct trade between India and the rest of the world virtually impossible, while exports of raw cotton, rice and wheat to European markets increased and Indian industrial centres cut production to a minimum. The Indian economy was being transformed into an agricultural support system for British manufacturing capitalism, and the British introduced major changes in the land ownership which helped create a free market in land and labour at the beginning of the 19th century.

From 1848 to 1856 the British conquered eight Indian states, a direct cause of the Indian rebellion in 1857 known in British history as the Mutiny. In 1858 the British government assumed control of Indian affairs. More land was opened to British industry, as British railways, docks and irrigation projects began to 'modernise' the country. By 1876 India had become the centre of British trade in the Far East, providing a market for British products, a source of regular income from monopolies and taxes, and a profitable field of investment. It was also a vital strategic base.

In Britain the public presentation of imperialism centred on the idea of a 'civilising mission', suggesting a progressive, humanitarian motive for the exploitation of India's resources and exercise of political control. Social conditions in India could be seen to justify the need for British rule: Caste, communalism, illiteracy, poverty, purdah and 'the position of women' were grouped together as problems — obstacles to mobility, education, employment, political rights and progress in general. Most British liberals and feminists knew very little about the situation in India under British rule. Some supported demands for political independence. Very few British women living in India openly questioned the British presence.

## British Women In India

British women began to arrive in India at the end of the 17th century as wives of EIC employees and, after 1750, the EIC actively encouraged single women to look for husbands. For the British in India in the 1920s society had not changed much since Victorian times. They governed two thirds of India; each district had its military cantonment, its 'civil lines' with the town or village 'beyond the pale'. A look at memoirs of British women who saw India as home shows that it could be difficult to fit into a colonial way of life. They were expected to do very little in the way of work and as one memsahib recalled:

> They never entirely integrated with India and this was terribly important as far as the whole ethos of the Raj was concerned. The men were very closely integrated but not their servants and we met a great many Indians, and some of us undoubtedly made a very close study of India and the Indian customs, but once you stepped inside the home you were back in Cheltenham or Bath.[1]

> In this context, integration meant fitting in with a colonial social structure rather than with Indian society. As in middle-class Victorian Britain, men had work while women's place was in the home.[2]

Not all British women shared this attitude. For example, in the 1860s and 70s Flora Annie Steel shared her husband's work in welfare and education, battled with the government of India when she disagreed with its policies, and was eventually made an Inspector of Schools in the Punjab. She gathered traditional folktales from the people and translated and published them in English, as *Tales of the Punjab*. Hers is an exceptional story, and Mrs Steel was one of the few British colonial wives who refused to sacrifice personal ambition to the conventions of British society in India. Mary Carpenter, who worked in India from 1866 in the field of women's education, noted how 'unconventional' behaviour met with disapproval and even to accusations of letting down the European race and the empire. Recent work on white women in colonial societies has shown how they have been left out of historical accounts and, at the same time, held responsible for causing racial conflict and 'losing the empire'. It has been argued that while the structures and institutions of imperial governments were established and maintained by men, British women had a more flexible and responsible approach towards being in India. The involvement of British women in Indian welfare work, particularly in education and medicine, began in the early 1800s. The first British school for Indian girls, run by the London Missionary Society, was set up in 1818. By 1901, 467 primary and 5,628 secondary schools had been established.

In a survey conducted by the Cambridge Centre of Asian Studies on British women in India, 102 women responded to the request for information about their lives. Of these, 21 had been involved in welfare work. While these women were unconventional by contemporary standards, they spoke in support of British rule and clearly took pride in what they saw as its achievements.[3]

Some personal accounts by women living as colonial wives show an alienation which was rarely revealed in public.

Frieda Haswirth, a Swiss painter married to an Indian sugar manufacturer from a state in Orissa which had maintained its independence, found herself excluded from conservative white society because she had stepped over carefully preserved racial boundaries.[4]

In her autobiography, Haswirth wrote critically about European attitudes to empire and in particular, the ideas of racial superiority that were so important to many people she met. During her journey to Bombay by ship she had been advised on various aspects of home management, including the need to put padlocks on the kitchen cupboards to stop her servants from stealing. She decided not to start her new life by acting like a typical memsahib, and when her supplies began to disappear and bills increased, she asked Indian friends what she should do. She was told that most servants working for Indian families earned half as much as she paid; if she stopped trying to be a liberal employer, she would get better service. For Frieda Haswirth, it took time to fit into a different way of life as part of an Indian family in the 1920s.

Both Flora Annie Steel and Frieda Haswirth probably would have been described as 'odd women' since they did not conform to contemporary notions about how white women in colonial countries should live. After the 1914-19 war, however, increasing numbers of European women in India joined women's organisations; there were more social welfare and opportunities for educated women with professional skills to work in many parts of the world, where health, education and welfare were becoming a matter for government intervention.

## Welfare Workers

From the 1860s, British imperial policy was said to have changed due to a concern for the 'the material and moral progress of India'. But progress and development continued to be manipulated in the interests of Britain in alliance with Indian co-operators, and demands for radical reform continued to be made in India and in England. By the 1930s, Rajani Palme Dutt estimated that for every 3,840 people living in 'British India', there was only one hospital bed available.[5]

Indian activists' demands for government spending on public services had been largely ignored, and most social work was privately funded. When women's organisations in England began to take up the same issues, their work was welcomed by the government. The National Association for Supplying Female Medical Aid to the women of India and the Lady Chelmsford All India League for Maternity and Child Welfare trained women in medicine, and in 1923 they joined with the Victoria Memorial Scholarship Fund and the Women's Medical Service for India in offering a centralised service funded by charitable donations. They took a travelling exhibition around the country to publicise its services. They recommended more government spending on social welfare, as the scope of their work was limited, due partly to the lack of resources and state support.

Although such organisations provided much needed services and funding, their position as 'benevolent imperialists' brought them into conflict with Indian ways of working: they criticised Indian midwives for using what they regarded as dangerously unskilled methods and refusing to take part in training schemes. The 'we know best what you need' attitude of reformers, which in England was used against working-class women, was magnified by racial prejudice in some records of work in India. Progress may have been made in terms of service provision for women, but they were run along the lines of English 'rescue work' organisations in the sense that 'help' was to be given to 'disadvantaged' women.

Attempts were made to carry out research into the conditions of Indian workers: one survey,[6] compiled by two British women social workers attached to the National Christian Council of India, Burma and Ceylon, was intended as a guide for welfare organisations, to identify industrial problems and planning reforms. Although the result, published in 1930, contained useful information on pay and conditions, the lack of economic and political critique and emphasis on social problems limited its usefulness.

They argued that conditions for industrial workers were clearly in need of improvement, but that this would take time. They claimed that antiquated habits, ignorance and illiteracy stood in the way of change, creating 'suspicion, prejudices and sheer inertia'. It was unlikely, they said that workers would organise successfully in trade unions because of the 'difficulty of translating western forms into methods comprehensible to eastern thought'. If the workers had problems organising, however, they seem to have solved them without experience in British-style trade unionism. Later in the survey:

> The present time is not normal; industrial unrest is a menace almost everywhere, and in the great cotton centre of Bombay it is a positive peril to industry. Representatives of all parties agree in ascribing this situation largely to political and alien influence and regarding it more as part of the world-communist agitation than as directly caused by industrial relations.[7]

This refusal to recognise the growth of resistance to British rule seems to have been a problem which reached crisis point before it was faced. Agatha Harrison, who worked with the Indian Conciliation Group in support of Indian independence and for mutual understanding, thought the industrial and political situation had nothing to do with nationalist challenge to British rule. She wrote:

> This whole situation is so big and bewildering and agonising; you feel you are on the edge of a volcano. Some see it, some pretend not to and walk warily over the very thin crust. Others don't see anything at all.[8]

As someone who preferred to keep out of the political limelight, Agatha Harrison is remembered for persuading people on opposite sides to meet and co-operate in England and in India during the 1930s and 40s. Her association with India began in 1929 as assistant to Beryl Power, a member of the Royal Commission on Labour in India. She spent six months in India making contact with Indian industrialists, trade union and labour officials and political leaders, and was successful in arranging informal contact with the Commission. When the India Conciliation Group formed at the end of 1931 to facilitate communication between British officials and Indian political leaders, funding for Agatha Harrison's position as secretary came from the Gandhian industrialist, G D Birla. In January 1932 she wrote to Gandhi:

The letters are arriving regularly from India, and we are making good use of them. Krishna Menon sees the press is kept informed, and I cover the religious press, and see that Mr Croft of the India Office, Lord Irwin etc. sees all that is sent. I am working closely with the various groups, and seeing how we can co-ordinate the various activities and see that no gaps are left.[9]

Part of her work involved contact with Indian women's organisations. She corresponded regularly with well-known figures including Amrit Kaur and Sarojini Naid, and attended the All-India Women's Conference throughout the 1930s. While she was not active in campaigns for women's rights as such, her work in the Indian Conciliation Group and the Women's International League for Peace and Freedom — where she raised the question of British rule in India and was instrumental in organising WILPF support for Indian nationalism — made a significant contribution to the movement for international cooperation among women.

## Reform and Social Change

In Britain, the entry of women into parliament from the 1920s provided women with a more public platform for international issues and foreign affairs. Some women MPs felt that government policy on Empire had failed to take women's interests into account but that British women now had an opportunity to make amends for what was seen as official negligence.

In 1919, the Government of India had passed administrative responsibility for some matters of provincial government to Indian officers. The situation was to be reviewed in ten years' time with a view to gradual reform in the direction of self-government. In November 1927 the exclusively British Commission of enquiry, known as the Simon Commission, was formed. Its authority was resisted strongly in India by boycott pickets, industrial strikes and militant action — which was played down in international news reports. In England, feminist MP Eleanor Rathbone and the 'equal rights' organisation NUSEC (the National Union of Societies for Equal Citizenship) called a meeting to discuss conditions in India for women, and whether anything could be done to help. (This initiative was partly inspired by the book *Mother India*, by an American, Katherine Mayo, whose main theme was how Indian women were oppressed by Indian men.) As Eleanor Rathbone said:

Like other movements, it [the women's movement] is becoming more international, especially within the bounds of the British Empire. Some of us are imperialists; some of us are not. But so long as imperialism is an inescapable fact, its responsibilities are also an inescapable fact, and these for the women of this country include the welfare of all those women in India and the East.[10]

An ex-governor of Bengal, Lord Lytton, emphasised that British women had a responsible and positive part to play in dealing with social problems in India, and NUSEC approached the Simon Commission, suggesting that women should be brought onto this body which had been criticised strongly in India and in England because of its all-British composition. Indian feminist Hannah Sen commented:

India remains a subject of keen interest and became one also of speculation when the Simon Commission opened to the British women a wide vista of influence and service. Their gratuitous individual members of the Commission came to be regarded somewhat as a feminine version of British Imperialism and as disguised efforts to perpetuate India's enslavement.[11]

The NUSEC attempt to make an alliance with Indian women's organisations went further, arranging a national women's conference in preparation for a proposed survey into the position of women in India. The conference was chaired by Eleanor Rathbone and took place at Caxton Hall in October 1929; Indian women were invited in the capacity of 'advisors'. Eleanor Rathbone's recently published pamphlet, *Has Katherine Mayo Slaughtered Mother India* was on the tables. When the Indian women drew attention to the undemocratic way the conference had been organised and other points to do with the arrangement of business, they were apparently ruled out of order. When they raised the issue of the pamphlet, based as it was on Katherine Mayo's opinions about India and Indian women, there was a heated discussion on the relationship between British and Indian women. Dhanvanthi Rama Rao said English women had failed to understand the Indian women's movement. She put very little value on the pamphlet but protested at the conduct of the conference. She was one of a group including Hannah Sen and Dorothy Jinarajadas who wrote to the *Guardian*, dissociating themselves and Indian women's organisations from the proposed NUSEC survey of 'women of India':

It is truly regrettable that at this critical time, when representative Indian women in London are desirous of establishing friendly relations with the British women's Organisations, they should be treated in this high-handed and unsympathetic way... we have had too many enemies in the guise of friends and do not mean to take any more risks.[12]

Several organisations including the Women's Freedom League, the British Commonwealth League and the Indo-British Mutual Welfare League disaffiliated from the conference and the NUSEC survey lost much support. In 1930 it was published as *The Key of Progress*, with government approval, and made no suggestion for broadening its principles to include equal rights for all women.

A more constructive contribution to co-operation between British and Indian women's organisations appeared in the *Bulletin of the Indian Women's Movement*. The first issue was published in May 1934 in England by a group of women from various organisations, including the Six Point Group, the Women's International League for Peace and Freedom, and others who had disagreed with NUSEC's position. Material for publication was sent from India by members of a liaison group including representatives of the Women's Indian Association, the All-India Women's Conference and the National Council of Women in India, to provide a source of information for anyone who was interested in reports of meetings, campaigns and action being taken by Indian women.[13]

The newsletter also offered an alternative to inaccurate reports of events in India in the British press; this had been taken up in an article on International Sisterhood by the Irish feminist Margaret Cousins, who lived in India, took an active interest in the Indian women's movement and organised the first All-India Women's Conference in 1927. On her travels through Europe as international representative of the women's Indian Association, she noted:

The specialised viewpoint of Christian missionaries; the political and commercial vested interests of England, the exaggerations and untruths of 'Mother India' have all combined to draw generalised pictures of India so false, so damaging to its reputation that I often found myself flaming in passionate revolt against the questions that were put to me.[14]

She asked why, when every country had its own social problems, India was singled out in this way. There were women on legislative councils, over 100 women on municipal and local governing boards, 80 women magistrates, while in France and Switzerland women did not have the vote. For Eleanor Rathbone, the idea of 'equal rights' meant (as Lord Lytton had suggested) that British women as well as men had a responsibility to improve conditions for everyone living under British rule in India. In her view:

> It cannot be right that British men should be able and expected to express views and exercise influence, while British women are asked to keep their hands off.[15]

In preparation for the next round of reforms to be implemented in the Government of India Act of 1935, a group of British feminists formed the British Committee for Indian Women's Franchise in April 1933, in order to put pressure on the government to improve Indian women's voting rights. They saw their role as intermediary between the British Parliament and the organised Indian women's movement. In Eleanor Rathbone's notes outlining points to be made in the case, she emphasised that until after the First World War British women had no vote and therefore no influence on imperial policy; this might be the last time before the government was forced to pull out of India that British women could have a say on how to improve conditions and take some responsibility for what was being done. She wrote to Amrit Kaur (who would become one of the first women in the new Indian Government) to support their efforts and sought to separate the women's cause from the nationalist struggle:

> I know you feel inclined merely to 'non-co-operate'. But will you allow me to say, from my knowledge of public opinion here, that I am afraid that would produce very little effect. You would be merely lumped in the public mind with Congress and they will draw no distinction between the women's protest and the Congress protest, which is anticipated beforehand and so discounted.[16]

The most significant change made in the 1935 Act was that a tiny minority of the Indian population (10% men; 0.06% women) could now vote for members to sit on administrative councils in provincial government, and after the 1937 elections the Indian congress party formed local government bodies with limited powers. Indian nationalists had agreed to co-operate with the reforms, but at the same time the Act was designed to give few concessions. In Amrit Kaur's opinion:

Decisions have been arrived at which, with the best political verbiage, can in no way be camouflaged into being ostensibly for the benefit of India.[17]

Eleanor Rathbone persisted in her criticism of activists who, as she saw it, were abandoning the women's movement to 'take part in the political struggle'. It seemed to her that the cause of women's liberation in India was being held back, because the most politically active women preferred the tactics of civil disobedience to gradual reform. She believed that the British government could act as a liberating force in India by introducing social legislation to release women from the restrictions and abuses of male dominance; but political change had to be imposed by an elected government and non-parliamentary action was not, in her view, 'practical politics'.[18]

In the context of the kind of changes that some activists were calling for, the 1935 Act must have seemed insignificant. According to *Stri Dharma,* the Women's Indian Association journal:

India is waging four struggles in one — the individual struggle against the forces of violence and hatred in the individual, secondly, the economic exploitation of the Indian markets which can be self-contained, thirdly, the struggle against the undesired domination of an alien nation, and fourthly, the struggle against warfare by armaments and killing, such as has disgraced western civilisation.[19]

As far as social reform was concerned, it seemed that projects begun by Indian campaigners had been ignored while the efforts of British reformers were hailed as great achievements. In a letter to Ann Caton of NUSEC, Dr Muthulakshmi Reddi pointed out that social change was still effectively blocked by the government's refusal to consider proposals and its concern to maintain good relations with reactionary sections of Indian society. The effects on social welfare services had been disastrous as a result of the government's policy of 'utter indifference, neutrality and sometimes direct opposition to all our social reform measures.[20]

The 'rescue work' feminists' solution was to involve women in imperial policy making rather than to campaign for an immediate transfer to political power to a national government. The publicity given to India's 'social problems' led to British rule being seen as a positive alternative to

Indian patriarchy. While this was undoubtedly the prevailing view among British feminists, there were those with a wider outlook on British rule in India and the meaning of equal rights for women.

## Feminism and Co-operation

Like many Western women, Margaret Cousins lived and worked in India as a teacher. She and Annie Besant, both veterans of the Irish suffrage and Home Rule for Ireland campaigns, also supported the movement for Indian self-determination. They were part of the Women's Indian Association delegation who met the Secretary Of State for India in 1917 to discuss the question of Indian women's voting rights. While their role in this kind of action may have been overstated because of their position as well-known feminists and Irish nationalists in England, they made valuable contributions to the Indian movements for political independence and women's rights.

In 1917 Annie Besant was elected president of the Indian National Congress party in recognition for work done in the campaigns for Indian Home Rule in 1915 and 1916. She disagreed, however, with the future civil disobedience and non-co-operation tactics, because popular leaders would be unable to control mass action. In her book *India, Bond or Free* she wrote: 'my own hope is to see an Indo-British Commonwealth of Coloured and White Nations' in which each supplied the others' defects: the materialism of the west and the spiritualism of the east combining two great civilisations with complementary traditions in philosophy, art and literature'.[21]

Before that could be a reality, though, Home Rule for India had to be negotiated by political representatives, rather than won through a national struggle for democracy.

In her efforts to build support in England for the independence movement, Annie Besant formed the Home Rule for India British Auxiliary in 1912. In 1923 it was renamed the Commonwealth of India League, and from 1928, under the direction of future High Commissioner for India V K Krishna Menon, became a more radical force working for complete self-determination. By education and action designed to break through ignorance and prejudice, it would appeal to British working-class people, trade unionists and others involved in the wider labour movement. Two British feminists and left-wingers, Ellen Wilkinson and Monica Whately, were among the India League activists who undertook a 'fact-finding' visit to India in 1932, supported by the Indian National Congress.

At a time of high unemployment and growing poverty in the industrial north of England, Scotland and Wales, cheap food and raw materials imported from different parts of the British Empire were vital resources to ease the economic situation. In the 1930s the British government authorised a firm line on law and order to deal with political activism in Britain, and with 'extremists' in India. At the same time, there was a liberal view that if elected government in England also governed parts of India, people in Britain could not ignore what was happening there. The India League planned to publish a report, based on the 'fact-finding' visit, which would make it clear that the methods of British rule in India would be intolerable if used against British people.

The delegation set off to look at different topics including industry and agricultural poverty, law and order, prison conditions, nationalism in rural areas, and the attitudes of British people in India. When they left England in August 1932, there had been two 'Round Table Conferences' held in London to discuss constitutional reform. Gandhi had been invited to represent the Congress Party, but there was no settlement and he was arrested on his return to India at the end of 1931. Civil disobedience, in which vast numbers of women were involved, was accelerated. Emergency measures were put into operation and allegations of atrocities were denied by the Secretary of State. It was admitted officially that the extent of government repression could be described as 'drastic', while in public, conciliation and co-operation were presented as the aim of imperial policy.[22]

With INC support, the India League representatives travelled through all the provinces under British government. They met a wide range of people in towns and in rural areas, and recorded statements on different aspects of social, political and economic conditions. From information given to the IL it seemed that conditions had deteriorated since the civil disobedience campaign in 1931, when many people had been imprisoned and property confiscated or destroyed. The possibility of a negotiated agreement had been overtaken by an emergency situation in which arbitrary laws were being issued and enforced on grounds of 'peace and good government'.[23]

Police were authorised to arrest and detain suspected persons, take possession of buildings, control transport services, impose government services, censor and search, and collect fines from whole villages or districts for tax arrears. The IL's description of conditions in some areas suggested military occupation and open warfare: villages blockaded, supplies taken, curfews imposed, special courts set up, and identity checks instigated to control people's movements.[24]

The extent of civil resistance was evidently much wider than reported outside India, especially away from major towns. Women activists faced violence and intimidation, and there were complaints of sexual violence by police officers of all ranks. A government officer admitted:

> The treatment meted out to women civil resisters is intended to frighten them away by making such participation dangerous to their person and their self-respect.[25]

Government officers were clearly anxious to present a different picture to that given by the IL reporters. In Bombay they were told that all Congress broadcasts were untrue and that police never beat women; however from the number of signed statements they obtained from women in different areas, the IL concluded that on the basis of circumstantial evidence and the widespread nature of the allegations, attacks on women by the police was one of the unpublicised realities of British rule in India.

The IL's report, published as *The Condition of India*, was banned by the Government. It conveyed a striking impression of a 'police raj' which had existed, according to some accounts, even before the 'state of emergency' in 1932. In the IL's opinion:

> In dealing with the civil disobedience movement and other allied activities the police in India have used excessive force and adopted methods which are indefensible.[26]

In 1934 the IL began to publish *India Today,* a monthly paper intended to give an alternative, non-official, picture of what was happening. By March 1936, reporters noted:

> ... no abatement of working-class unrest, no improvement in the lot of the peasantry, no slackening of the official reign of terror.[27]

The IL's work was an important part of agitation against British rule and in support of national liberation movements from the 1920s to the 1940s. This kind of solidarity work has been pushed into the background of British labour history, and also needs to be recognised as part of feminist history. Ellen Wilkinson, for example, is remembered for her work in Jarrow as an MP in the 1930s and for raising women's issues in parliament, but her views on British rule in India have been less well documented. In 1929, when Eleanor Rathbone asked British women's organisations to sign a letter to the *Times* about the need for a new law to raise the legal age of marriage and consent in India, Ellen Wilkinson replied:

> I feel that a word from Gandhi could not only do a thousand times more good than any letter in the *Times*, but such a letter could be positively harmful in so far as it seems to press a reform upon them by an alien race.[28]

> Her India League work is given little attention in historical accounts, as are the political writings of women like Joan Beauchamp, Elinor Burns and Sylvia Pankhurst on the subject of British imperialism.[29]

Sylvia Pankhurst is well known for her involvement in the suffrage movement, the East London workers' Socialist Federation, the 'Hands off Russia' campaign and against the Italian invasion of Ethiopia in 1935. Her book *India, The Earthly Paradise* was published in Bombay in 1926 while in the same year, Annie Besant's *India, Bond or Free*, was published in London. Both criticised British rule, arguing that imperialist exploitation had disrupted democratic development in economic, social and political life, and that the so-called benefits of foreign industrial capitalism had been limited by the over-riding interests of Europe, creating the conditions of 'under-development'.

Sylvia Pankhurst's book is one of the few contemporary works by British feminists to be written from a socialist perspective about government plans to foster economic growth in the sugar industry, she comments:

> Observing that the peasant sugar-cane growers of Madras and Mysore were able to get a higher price for their 'gur' than the price ruling in Fiji and Mauritius, it was decided that the price in southern India should be increased 'until the market for 'gur' is overdone'. They advised that a glut in cane should be created to force the growers to sell more cheaply, and so test whether capital could earn dividends by setting up a sugar cane factory. If the cultivators should not be able to make even a bare living at the lower price, if they should fall into debt and difficulty, perhaps lose their holdings; if they should finally give up the attempt to grow cane — then the capitalists would know that their money would be more profitably invested in other directions. To facilitate that discovery some poor peasants would have lost their all. Such are capitalist methods.[30]

In Sylvia Pankhurst's view, British government changes in land and labour had accentuated class and communal divisions and increased exploitation. While an end to British rule was essential for Indian democratic development, in her vision of an international socialism, it was one step on the road to liberation.

She was also interested in the impact of British imperial policy on Indian social life, and in the implications for women, in particular, of changes in legislation. She noted that the British idea of progress could in fact help to destroy traditional democratic institutions: for example, according to customary law in some places including Assam and Malabar, property was vested in the female line and could not be sold by an individual man even if he was responsible for managing it.

Divorce might be allowed by local custom but was impossible under Brahmanic law, and in cases where there may have been some conflict, Sylvia Pankhurst saw that British courts could accentuate the parts of Indian law and practice that penalised women. In cases of doubt, women were generally discriminated against by British legislators because they wanted to avoid conflict with powerful sections of Indian society.

While some British feminists persisted in seeing all Indian women as a class suffering under male domination, she took a different view of the problems to do with 'traditional customs' and providing social welfare:

> The Bombay census authorities complained of young wives being put in outhouses and sheds during their confinements. Whether the family was able to provide any better place of quiet and privacy for them is not stated. The Health Commissioner says the state cannot afford to provide the requisite skilled aid for mothers and infants. He appeals to the public to subscribe to voluntary agencies for this purpose... Its meaning is: the masses are too poor to provide the necessary care for their mothers and infants. We cannot alleviate their poverty. We intend to govern the masses. They must pay for being governed. It costs so much to maintain the government that the government cannot afford to provide social ameliorations of the prevailing poverty.[31]

Such criticism of the system was rare, and after 1919 liberal-minded British women began to take responsibility for the 'wrongs' of government policy by working on welfare projects; for good intentions were not enough to tackle broad-based inequalities and harsh facts of political control, so the possibility of significant change was limited. Constructive relationships between individuals, opportunities for training and increased services did make a contribution to welfare provision but, as Muthulakshmi Reddi pointed out in a letter to Ann Caton of NUSEC in 1929:

> We women have come to realise that a foreign government has no sympathy with the legitimate aspirations of the people, and can never actively help in mending our defective social system. Dominion status is granted, there can be no real social and moral progress.[32]

British rule in India became a complex question of equal rights for Eleanor Rathbone. She saw her role as one of taking responsibility for the regrettable consequences of mistaken imperial policy. The mistake was not, however, in British domination of India, but in bad government; and this could be corrected if women were given some power to decide government policy. It was assumed that British women could protect the interests of Indian women more effectively than if women's issues were left to men — either Indian politicians or British government — and it was clearly difficult for some feminists to accept the views of Indian activists with years of political experience. The conviction that the British women's movement had a blueprint for a tried and tested means of achieving liberation, which could be taught to women in different circumstances, was based on mistaken and patronising ideas about women, race, history and freedom.

It is difficult to assess the impact of political writing, and in the case of Annie Besant, Sylvia Pankhurst and other women who wrote critiques of British imperialism, their work is unlikely to have reached a wide audience. The India League's agitation and propaganda through distributing information and organising events was probably effective in political education, and their women's committee had connections with groups in trade unions and co-operative guild branches throughout Britain. According to a report in *About India*, December 1942:

> In the Co-op movement the women's Guilds have led the way, both by their campaign and their full support for a National Government now.[33]

The study of these women who worked in the context of British rule in India shows that more needs to be done to give a clearer picture of social relations between British and Indian women, individually and in organisations, in the period before India regained political independence. In the decades before 1947 colonial wives played their part in maintaining

British rule in India and welfare workers carried on with their work against a background of increasing political tension and widespread unrest. A small number of British women in India recognised the need for conciliation, changes in British policy and the rights to national self-determination. In Britain, organisations like the India League, the Indian Conciliation Group, the women's International League for Peace and Freedom,

Feminist groups and labour movement organisations supported Indian calls for immediate national government. While the 'imperialist feminists' demanded a say in British imperial policy in order to promote Indian women's rights, they were unable to ignore the contradictions raised by Indian women. International sisterhood among British and Indian women was clearly more than a theoretical issue in the 1920s and 30s, and had some successes and some failures. It is a complex history of polarisation, co-operation, difference and friendship. The Indian women's movement asked British feminists for support rather than patronage, and in 1937 Margaret Cousins gave this advice to her British sisters:

> Study more, drop prejudices, and be ready and brave for changed valuations, changed ways and changed lives.[34]

# Notes

1.  Birdwood, V, quoted in Allen, C. (ed), *Plain Tales from the Raj, London, 1975*
2.  See, e.g. Callaway, H, *Gender, Culture and Empire,* Macmillan, 1987 Knapman, C, *White Women In Fiji: the Ruin of Empire?,* Allen and Unwin, 1987
3.  Lind, M.A. *The Compassionate Memberships: Welfare Activities of British Women in India,* 1900-47
4.  Hansmith, F. *A Marriage to India,* Hutchinson, 1931, pp 29- 30
5.  Dutt, R.P. *Guide to the Problem of India,* Gollancz, 1942, p.41
6.  Matheson, C. *Indian Industry Yesterday, Today and Tomorrow,* London, 1907
7.  Ibid
8.  Harrison, I. *Agathar Harrison: An Impression by her sister,* Allen and Unwin, 1956. p.65
9.  Harrison to Gandhi, January 29, 1932, London Society of Friends Temp Mss 41/1
10.  'Women's header,' July 13 1928
11.  'Stri Dharma', January 1930
12.  'Stri Dharma', December 1929
13.  Bulletin of the Indian Women's Movement, May 1984
14.  Cousins, M. 'International Sisterhood', Stri Dharma, December 1929
15.  ER to R. Subbaroyan, 8 January 1932, Rathbone Correspondence, Faucult Library
16.  ER to R.A. Kaur, 18 March 1933, Rathbone Correspondence
17.  Kaur, R.A., Women Under the New Constitution, Women: Our Cause, 1935, p.372
18.  ER to R. Subbaroyan, 9 April 1931, Rathbone Correspondence
19.  'Stri Dharma', April 1930
20.  Reddi, M. ER, 29th July 1931, Rathbone Corresp.
21.  Besant, A, *India, Bond or Free, Bombay, 1926, p.126*
22.  The Condition of India 1932, India League Publications
23.  ibid p.34
24.  ibid p.58
25.  ibid p.194
26.  ibid p.163
27.  'India Today', March 1936 p.3
28.  Wilkinson, E. to ER, Undated, Rathbone Corresp.
29.  See, e.g., Beauchamp, Joan, *British Imperialism in India* 1934; Burns, Elinor, *Colonial Series,* 1926; Pankhurst, Sylvia, *India: The Earthly Paradise,*
30.  Pankhurst, S. *India: the Earthly Paradise*, p.386
31.  Ibid p.209
32.  Reddi, M. to Ann Caton, 24 Feb, 1939
33.  'About India' IL Publications, December 1942, p.5
34.  Bulletin of the Indian Women's Movement, January 1937

# 6

# Middle-Class Anglo-Jewish Lady Philanthropists and Eastern European Jewish Women:
## the first national conference of Jewish women, 1902

*Rickie Burman*

## Introduction

The history of the Jewish community in Britain has to a large extent been that of Jewish men. Recent work has started to recover women's history by examining the changing role of immigrant Jewish women in economic and religious life, the provision of health care among Jewish women and the development of the Jewish women's movement prior to the 1930s[1]. This chapter brings together considerations of class, ethnicity and gender in a study of the philanthropic activities of Anglo-Jewish 'ladies' of the upper and middle classes in relation to working-class Jewish women of Eastern European background.

These topics are illustrated through an analysis of material taken from the first national Conference of Jewish Women, held in London in May, 1902. The papers given at this conference together with contemporary reports in the newspapers indicate, firstly, how the role of Jewish women philanthropists was defined within the Jewish community and perceived by the women themselves and, secondly, the influences which the middle class lady philanthropists sought to exert on women of the immigrant community. How far is it possible to identify a common view of Jewish womanhood, transcending the barriers of class and cultural background? To what extent were definitions of femininity within the Jewish community influenced by prevailing models in contemporary British society? The evidence from the conference, together with oral history interviews conducted with the children of Jewish immigrants in Manchester,[2] suggests that, despite the common bonds of religious affiliation and observance, for many Jewish women philanthropy represented the only point of intersection between two contrasting social and cultural worlds, the worlds of East End and West End, of immigrant woman and English lady.

By the end of the nineteenth century, the Jewish community in Britain was strongly divided by class, culture and religious background. On the one hand, there was an established Anglo-Jewish community, largely middle-class in composition and dominated by a small number of inter-related families, who combined an attachment to Jewish affairs with an equal dedication to British life and institutions.[3] After 250 years of settlement in Britain they had achieved a hard-won reputation for respectability, charitable self-sufficiency and exemplary civic pride. On the other hand, there was a growing Yiddish-speaking community of Jewish immigrants from Eastern Europe, predominantly working-class, who practised traditional religious observance and customs, and had little in common with their anglicised co-religionists.

It is estimated that at the height of this migration, 1881 to 1914, between 100,000 and 150,000 Jewish immigrants settled in Britain.[4] They sought to escape the poverty and oppressive conditions of life under the Tsarist regime in Russia; an inequitable system of military service, the fear of pogroms, and increasingly severe residential and economic overcrowding resulting from restrictions imposed on Jews.

In Britain, the majority of the immigrants settled in London's East End, but substantial numbers also settled in the growing industrial towns of the provinces, in particular Manchester, Leeds, Liverpool, Glasgow and Birmingham. They found work largely in small-scale economic enterprises as tailors, cabinet-makers, furriers and shoe-makers. Their arrival was greeted with mixed feelings by members of the established Anglo-Jewish community, which was already well integrated into British society by the time the influx of Eastern European immigrants reached its height. Highly sensitive to prevailing attitudes in the majority society, they felt threatened by the presence of so large and visible an immigrant population, which might place at risk their own hard won acceptance in British society. As the flow of migration gathered pace, they feared increasingly that it would exceed the capacity of their existing charitable institutions to absorb the immigrants and their own ability to control the community and shape its public image.

That these fears were not unfounded is indicated by the 1902 Commission on Alien Immigration, set up in direct response to agitation for restrictions on Jewish immigration. A special report in the *Jewish Chronicle* of 2 May 1902 provides a summary of the evidence given to the Commission by Arnold White, one of the most zealous campaigners for immigration restrictions: in his account of the 'mental and moral anatomy of the alien immigrant', which is specifically directed to Jewish immigrants, White lists 'good', 'doubtful' and 'bad' points, finding an adverse balance of vices and virtues. He also expresses concern that the charities established by the Anglo-Jewish community might serve as a magnet, attracting new immigrants. White's evidence emphasises the pressures to which members of the Anglo-Jewish community were subject and highlights the contingent nature of their own acceptance within the British establishment. They were made to feel that the behaviour of each individual immigrant was subject to critical scrutiny, and that any misdemeanour or negative attribute might be generalised from the individual to the Jewish community as a whole. While, for reasons of compassion as well as self-interest, they felt it incumbent on themselves to assist their poorer co-religionists and ensure that they did not become a burden on society, they had to avoid giving the impression of too open-handed or indiscriminate an approach to charitable work.

These tensions are apparent in the policies adopted by charities such as the London Jewish Board of Guardians (established 1859), which, although generally viewed as enlightened in relation to contemporary charitable institutions, stipulated that applicants for assistance were eligible only if they had been resident in Britain for at least six months. Moreover, it often advocated loans rather than outright relief to applicants. It also sent out letters to representative organisations in the immigrants' countries of origin seeking to discourage migration to Britain.

## Women's philanthropic organisations

While the same influences and concerns may be discerned in the philanthropic organisations with which women of the Anglo-Jewish community
were associated, to some extent they developed a distinctive approach to
charitable work, complementary to that of their male counterparts.

The involvement of individual Jewish women in philanthropy may be
traced back to 1662, when a number of women are known to have worked
as volunteers in charitable schools established by the community. In
London, prior to the establishment of the Jewish Board of Guardians, a
number of 'highly cultured, energetic gentlewomen' were already active
in assisting and visiting the East End poor, attending the Jews' Free School
and establishing Sabbath classes (*Jewish Chronicle* 21/2/02). In 1840
Louise Lady Rothschild initiated the first independent Jewish women's
philanthropic associations, the Jewish Ladies' Benevolent Loan Society
and the Ladies' Visiting Society.[5] Like other nineteenth century Anglo-
Jewish philanthropic organisations, these associations were strongly
influenced by the methods and approach of the Charity Organisation
Society, established by Octavia Hill. They sought to replace individual
acts of indiscriminate charity, which might encourage charitable
dependence, with a more organised approach which aimed to assist the
'deserving poor' and to foster a spirit of independence through thrift and
self-help.

A Ladies' Conjoint Visiting Committee was set up in London in 1882
under the auspices of the Jewish Board of Guardians, in recognition of
the importance of women's contribution in visiting the homes of Jewish
immigrants.[6] This served as a nucleus for new developments in the
Board's work, initiating a needlework training scheme (1884) and
Mothers' Meetings (1895) in the East End and assisting in the development of a Jewish Day Nursery. In 1887, following developments in
Manchester, Lady de Rothschild and Mrs Lionel Lucas placed a Yiddish-
speaking nurse at the disposal of the Visiting Committee for home visiting
in the East End, and in 1898 a Sick Room Help Society was established.

In addition to this work conducted under the auspices of the Board of
Guardians, a number of ladies were involved in the Jewish Association
for the Protection of Girls and Women (originally the Ladies' Society for
Prevention and Rescue Work), established as an autonomous body in 1885
by Lady Battersea. This Association set up a range of institutions
including homes to provide shelter for unmarried mothers and women

rescued from prostitution, and for 'friendless but respectable foreign girls', who might 'fall prey to the unscrupulous on arrival at the docks'.[7]

In Manchester, women's involvement in philanthropic endeavours followed a somewhat similar course, although here visiting and associated work was conducted independently of the Manchester Jewish Board of Guardians, and this facilitated the development of a more humane approach in these fields. The United Sisters' Maternity Society (founded c.1850), served as a precursor to the Manchester Jewish Ladies' Visiting Association, which was established in 1884 with the aim of popularising sanitary knowledge and inculcating habits of cleanliness and order among the Jewish poor. In addition to its core work specifically relating to health and hygiene, this Association ran a Sewing Department, established a Sick Nourishment Fund for convalescent women and children and initiated Social Evenings and Sabbath Services for Working Girls. Two other influential ladies' organisations in Manchester were the ladies' committee of the Manchester Jews' School and the Jewish Ladies' Clothing Society, established in 1853 to supply clothing to needy children in attendance at the School.

The Manchester Jewish Ladies' Visiting Association (JLVA) exemplifies two important aspects of the philanthropic work of Anglo-Jewish women. Firstly, it highlights the development of new initiatives by women, for women. A woman who began her involvement with the Association at the age of sixteen recalled:

> It was chiefly mothers. The feminine side. The women's side, women who were going to have babies ... They had a scheme whereby a woman during her confinement was allowed about a pint of milk a day and 2lbs of meat a week and laid out completely for the baby. This was the maternity side, you see. And this was not provided by any other organisation. Because the Board of Guardians would help a family with money, but this was specifically to look after the woman.[8]

The 'more personal social work', carried out by those associated with the JLVA[9] contrasted with the more authoritarian approach of the Jewish Board of Guardians, which, following the precepts of the Charity Organisation Society, subjected applicants to humiliating examinations in its zeal to restrict its largesse to the 'deserving poor'. The inception of the JLVA was viewed with suspicion and some hostility by that body, which feared an overlapping of functions that might encourage charitable dependence. However, once the Association had pledged not to dispense monetary relief, amicable relations were established and the Association served to strengthen the influence of those who wished to humanise the work of the Board, co-operating for example in the formation of a joint sub-committee (1913) to give a regular allowance to widows with young children.

The JLVA also illustrates the way in which philanthropic initiatives developed by the women of the Anglo-Jewish community mirrored, and in some cases influenced, developments in the wider society. The JLVA was modelled closely on the Manchester and Salford Ladies' Sanitary Association (later the Ladies' Health Society), and the precise means of contact can even be traced. One of the Association's founders, Mrs Lawrence Simmons, had been an active member for several years, bringing 'a wealth of experience to guide us in our first tentative steps' (JC 23/5/02). A report notes that she and the first Health Visitor, who had experience of visiting from Glasgow, were 'the only two people connected with the new charity, who had experience of visiting the poor with the object of educating them in matters of hygiene and not of bestowing alms'.[10]

## The First Conference of Jewish Women, 1902

It was Mrs Simmons who first proposed the idea of the Conference of Jewish Women, and other contributors to the Conference also played a prominent role in non-sectarian charities and women's organisations: the Conference President, Mrs N.L. Cohen, was active in promoting improved educational opportunities for women. Lily Montagu was a founder member of the National Organisation of Girls' Clubs and Lady Battersea was a pioneer in prison visiting, who had served both as President and as Vice-President of the National Union of Women Workers.

The 1902 Conference of Jewish Women served as a showcase for the philanthropic endeavours of Jewish women and the *Jewish Chronicle* hailed it as 'a landmark of progress achieved'. The paper judged the event to be of such significance that it printed full transcripts of the conference papers and initiated a series of weekly profiles on individual Jewish women philanthropists, which continued over five months. These articles provide valuable information about the activities of Jewish women and afford penetrating insights into how their role was perceived among the established Anglo-Jewish community.

The Conference took place on 13th and 14th May at the Portman Rooms in Baker Street, London, attended by over 800 ladies from all parts of Britain, although the majority were Londoners. The programme for the first day included papers on Jewish District Nursing, the Care of the Sick and Convalescent Poor, Women's Communal Work in Manchester, Organisation in Charitable Work and Preventive and Rescue Work. On the second day, delegates heard papers on Home-Worship in its relation to Social Work, Occupation and Recreation of our Work Girls, Care of Girls after School Life and Intercommunication and Cooperation of Communal Workers. Delegates were offered the opportunity to visit communal institutions, such as the Jews' Free School and the Jewish Board of Guardians, and the Conference was concluded by a 'brilliant' reception at the Grafton Galleries, attended by several hundred guests, including the Chief Rabbi and his wife.

The aim of the event was said to be to enable women workers from all parts of the country 'to meet and discuss matters concerning the spiritual, social and moral welfare of the community, and to interchange information as to various methods of communal work in London and the provinces.' These aims were subsequently taken up by the Union of Jewish Women, formed as a result of the Conference.

## The ideal of the Anglo-Jewish female philanthopist

In nineteenth century England, a key distinction was drawn between the arenas of the public and private, the workplace and the home, the former being a male province and the latter regarded as a protected female domain. With the development of capitalism and the growth of the domestic ideology under Evangelical influence, the separation widened between the two spheres and women became increasingly excluded from worldly affairs.[11] As more generally among the middle classes, women in the Anglo-Jewish community were assigned the role of spiritual guardians. It was their responsibility to preserve the sanctity of the home and family life and, through their influence, to try to counteract the polluting effect of the outside world upon their menfolk.

While the importance of women's influence was frequently stressed to legitimate their confinement to the domestic sphere, as the century progressed their sphere of operations gradually extended. It became seen as acceptable and even appropriate that lady philanthropists should venture from their own homes into the homes of the poor, with the aim of effecting changes by example and gentle persuasion. By the same token, the working-class Jewish immigrant women were regarded as having a crucial role within their own homes as the bearers of children and the informal educators of the next generation. The immigrant women therefore were perceived as an important target — as well as a natural constituency — for the socialising influences of the Anglo-Jewish lady philanthropists.

From the articles about the conference in the *Jewish Chronicle*, (*JC*) a distinct impression emerges of how the role and characteristics of Jewish women were perceived within the established Anglo-Jewish community. Jewish women are seen as earnest, sincere and modest, possessing moral strength and spiritual integrity, working selflessly and excelling in attention to detail. The selfless dedication evinced by the women is compared favourably with the more competitive self-aggrandisement encountered at male gatherings. One writer comments:

> If only it were possible for a Jewish Conference of Men to be carried through in a spirit of true earnestness, with a brave and single-hearted desire to face the truth, and without self-laudation (*JC* 30/5/02).

Implicit in this emphasis on women's 'earnestness', however, is a certain sense of amusement at the women taking themselves and their work so seriously, and hence a negation of the seriousness of their intentions. The Conference delegates were described as 'all looking and feeling very serious, and naturally impressed with the importance of the work in hand'. One commentator suggests that, while it was clear that the speakers at the conference 'intensely cared', there was perhaps a 'little lack of humour and lightness in their discourses' (*JC* 23/5/02). Another review highlights the role of the conference as a fashionable social event, and ends by placing the philanthropic workers back firmly in their more familiar contexts, among the tea-cups or as social hostesses:

> Jewesses are nothing if not sociable — thus the tea-room was largely frequented at the close of each afternoon meeting ... What a hum of voices, what gracious accents of welcome and encouragement to new and old workers in every field, what eager offers of help from London and the provinces greeted one on every side, accompanying the pleasant clatter of cups and saucers! How sincere were the congratulations from one to another, how true the expressions of gratitude towards the President, how inspiring the pressure of the hand that accompanied the pleasant word of thanks from the worker to the speaker! And then what a festive and joyous ending to those pleasant,

if tiring, days, was the social gathering in the Grafton Gallery where the brilliant President of the Conference became the genial hostess of the evening (*JC* 23/5/02).

The feminine virtues for which the lady philanthropists were praised were often regarded as going hand-in-hand with corresponding weaknesses. Thus this seemingly congratulatory review of women's progress carries a barb in the tail:

> They are rapidly showing that for certain departments of activity they are even better fitted than men. With the greater leisure and freedom from anxiety that they can command, they excel in attention to detail. In whatever they undertake they prove themselves in deadly earnest ... And it is trouble quite as much as intelligence which tells in the long run (*JC* 21/2/02).

Women were regarded as innately inferior in intelligence to men. They were perceived as unmethodical and unbusinesslike, lacking the ability to deal competently with financial matters or ideas on a large scale. Such shortcomings were seen as intrinsic to the female character and were rarely related to women's restricted access to information and experience. Women who manifested organisational skills were viewed as exceptional, as in the case of the Conference President, Mrs Nathaniel Louis Cohen (*JC* 7/3/02). Unlike most Jewish women of her class, Mrs Cohen had the advantage of a formal education at Queen's College, London (a college for ladies established in the mid 1880s). Implicit in the listing of her 'businesslike' attributes is a contrast with the characteristics generally associated with women. This is made still more explicit when she is commended as 'an admirable example of what a speaker should be, powerful, enthusiastic, eloquent yet restrained', never agitated or flurried and invariably courteous, as against the 'inaudibility of some speakers', and the 'unnatural raising of the voice' or 'shrill accents such as sometimes distress one at women's meetings' (*JC* 23/5/02).

The perceived opposition between male and female characteristics receives its most explicit statement in an obituary of Mrs Nathaniel Montefiore, the fifth daughter of Sir Isaac Goldsmid, who died aged 83 in 1902:

> Her intellectual gifts were very high, almost of a masculine order. She could master a difficult subject with ease; she had an extraordinary grasp of financial matters, and knew well the value of money and how

to spend it. There was an absence of feminine weakness in her composition; she was somewhat impatient of want of method, of ignorance of practical methods, and lack of thoroughness, all of which she stigmatised as defects more common to women than to men ... (*JC* 2/5/02).

The gender-based vocabulary used here accords closely with that obtaining more generally among the middle classes in nineteenth century England.[12] The normal sphere of activity for a middle-class woman was held to be the beautification of the home rather than the financial management of the establishment. As in the description of Mrs Cohen, this account overstates the difference in the actual activities of men and women, underestimating the level of administrative competence generally required for women of this class to manage their often sizeable households.

In general, ladies attempting to conduct their activities in a methodical and businesslike way are often presented as unnatural, as though they were trying to go against their own nature. They are seen as amusing when they are regarded as aping men; threatening when their activities appear to encroach on the public domain, hitherto perceived as the preserve of men. A parody of the conference, published in the *Jewish Chronicle* just before the event, depicts a group of 'lady workers', who meet and shake hands in 'rather a business-like manner'. They are armed with the outward trappings of male professionalism but this is seen as an affectation, alien to their more appropriate feminine concerns:

Most of them carry a small leather bag, well furnished with papers ... from the chatelaine at their waist depends a notebook, a pencil, a diary and similar useful articles. One of them consults a watch that is strapped in a leather band to her wrist, which adds to her businesslike appearance (*JC* 9/5/02 'Round the Tea Table').

Anglo-Jewish women had to overcome scepticism and resistance in order to pursue their philanthropic work[13]. In this same caricature, one lady is made to admit that 'many conferences might disturb family peace':

My husband used to grow enraged at my dashing through breakfast, forgetting to order luncheon, and leaving him to entertain the baby (*JC* ibid).

The editorial comment in the newspaper following the conference indicates a real concern that women's involvement in philanthropic work would draw them away from their domestic duties and lead them to neglect their husbands and fathers. The *Jewish Chronicle's* enthusiasm for the conference was not unconditional:

> If this abundant activity had been exercised at the expense of the duties which our wives and daughters owe primarily to their own homes, there would be small cause for congratulation. But the entire business of this week's conference may stand as proof that the most charming companions and efficient helpmeets are just those women who find relaxation in public work from the constant call of domestic worries (*JC* 16/5/02).

The Conference of Jewish Women was acclaimed by the editor of the *Jewish Chronicle* as 'a tremendous revelation to the community of its latent spiritual forces' (*JC* 16/5/02). Despite the practical nature of the work often involved in activities such as health care, district visiting or rescue work, their philanthropic endeavours were generally regarded as in keeping with women's spiritual nature and domestic mission,[14] and this had an important implication. Through their involvement in philanthropy, women were enabled to extend the scope of their activities in the public realm, without appearing to threaten the established structure of gender relations by encroaching on male-defined territory.

The gradual extension of women's role in this way was, for the most part, not pursued the lady philanthropists as a conscious objective. The Conference President was careful to make explicit her acceptance of the prevailing division of labour:

> A line of demarcation exists, and, I think, usefully exists, between the field that is particularly women's work and the field that is particularly men's work. For, without being solitary in our respective furrows, a clear understanding helps us to concentrate our energies on ploughing our own particular furrow and trying to do full justice to it. And also, I think it helps a mutual recognition of the fact that the lives and work of men and women are each the complement of the other (*JC* 16/5/02).

Mrs Cohen accepts that men and women have different strengths but she indicates that this does not mean that they cannot make a contribution of equal value. She goes on to define more closely what she perceives as the appropriate division of labour:

> It seems to me that women's special field is detail work. The larger questions with wide economic bearings, such for instance, as the

Housing Question, should, I think, be grappled with by men, and we may reasonably hope that problem will be effectually grappled with, when all the Borough Councils realise their very ample powers. But while men are forming measures to make overcrowding illegal and so gradually abate the huge rents and force a certain measure of dispersion in the too-densely crowded quarters, women can foster appreciation of decent quarters by their visits to the homes ... (*JC* ibid)

This indicates a development in the definition of women's role. For while Mrs Cohen accepts that women lack the power and resources to effect political and economic change, her words demonstrate an acute awareness of contemporary political questions and the connection between 'secular' questions and the accepted sphere of operations for women. Over the previous fifty years important changes had taken place in women's role. The *Jewish Chronicle* noted that the new century would be remembered as:

one in which women quietly and unostentatiously, but very surely, have proved their right to be regarded as the equal of men in many matters where formerly they had no voice, or at any rate, no official voice (*JC* 21/2/02).

Despite scepticism from 'captious critics who have jeered at the philanthropy of society ladies as the newest and smartest amusement, and suggested that "slumming' was but the caprice of the hour', women had shown that they could carry out work 'in all sincerity and in no dilettante fashion'. The conference could therefore be said to represent 'a definite goal reached, and ... a stepping-stone to still greater achievement' (*JC* ibid).

## Make them English women

Prochaska has identified some of the varied and often complex motives which drew 19th century English women into philanthropic work.[15] Like their non-Jewish counterparts, middle-class Jewish women became engaged in charitable endeavours to occupy their own time in a productive way, and to achieve a sense of self-worth and significance. For some women, philanthropy represented an escape route from 'the formality and enforced idleness of middle-class family life' and 'an obvious outlet for self-expression'. At the same time, sincere compassion and a genuine desire to 'do good', to better the lot of working-class Jewish women, were important motives. A further objective, implicit in most philanthropic work at the time, was the desire to improve the moral values and way of life of the poor;[16] in the words of one speaker at the Conference, 'to help not only materially, but morally to endeavour to improve the general condition' (JC 16/5/02). In the case of Jewish philanthropists, however, the moral and socialising role of philanthropy was further underscored by their concern to achieve the anglicisation of the foreign Jewish immigrants and their children, and in the case of the women, to inculcate values which would enable them to conform to English models of femininity.

To one speaker, the female philanthropist represented 'the good angel' to the families she befriended. Her task was to arouse in them the desire to help themselves; to talk of the value of education, the beauty of industry, what children owed to their parents, religion, race and fellow-creatures; to try to make them 'an honour to Judaism' and 'potentially good citizens'; to see the children were apprenticed to a good trade and that their spare time was spent in an elevating rather than a degrading way by lending them good books, which she could then discuss with them.

A range of means were employed to influence the behaviour of the daughters of Jewish immigrants. Measures were taken to inculcate virtues, such as cleanliness, thrift and good housewifery, and steps taken to discourage perceived negative aspects of immigrant life, such as the overcrowding of particular occupations, prostitution and dependence on charitable aid.

### Cleanliness

Cleanliness and tidiness were frequently mentioned as tackled particularly effectively by the Jewish Ladies' Visiting Association in Manchester. Here, a health visitor (by 1902, three health visitors) was employed to undertake an intensive programme of district visiting, advising immigrant housewives and distributing carbolic soap and powder, and leaflets translated into Yiddish. The advantages of employing Jewish Visitors, who spoke the language of the immigrants and might be more sensitive to their values and practices were emphasised by Margaret Langdon, who began her career in philanthropy by accompanying Manchester Corporation Health Visitors on their rounds. In the Jewish areas of Strangeways and Cheetham, she recalls, a large number of the households were:

> Very, very untidy. The houses looked messy. They also put out their bed linen, hung it out of their windows. Now the health visitors

thought that dreadful, and I had to explain to them that abroad it would have been thought very unhealthy not to air your bedding.[17]

She pointed out to the Health Visitors that, while the houses might appear untidy, they had a much lower incidence of infant diarrhoea, attributing this to the observance of Jewish dietary laws:

They keep their milk and meat pans separate, and that really forces them to wash properly. They wash everything under the tap.

The Association appreciated the importance of improving housing conditions as well as standards of housewifery, and exerted pressure on the local authorities to correct defects in housing or sanitation. In 1892 it reported that, owing to its representations, 'some of the worst back-to-back houses have now, by orders of the Corporation, been structurally altered, so as to remove entirely the evils complained of', and the following year, it drew the attention of the City Health Authorities to the need for erecting public baths and wash houses, noting 'the great difficulties under which the poor labour, when every drop of water has to be fetched from a stand-pipe in a somewhat distant street or court.'[18]

The children of immigrants often describe their mothers constantly cleaning and scrubbing, in a valiant yet hopeless battle against bugs and rodents. Yet, with the notable exception of the Manchester Association, little sensitivity is demonstrated by the Anglo-Jewish ladies' philanthropic organisations to the conditions of life or the cultural differences which made the virtues of cleanliness and tidiness difficult for the immigrants or irrelevant in their struggle to survive. A profile of Mrs Herman Tuck, the founder of the North London Grocery Fund, which collected shillings from the wealthy on a weekly basis to provide parcels for the needy, notes how the recipients ('aged men, sad-looking women, poverty-stricken children'), were taught passing lessons in politeness and cleanliness when receiving their bounty. The men were reminded to doff their caps and any persons arriving unwashed were warned that they would receive only soap next time (*JC* 30/5/02). A similar picture is drawn of the girls' Work Rooms, established by the London Jewish Board of Guardians, over which Mrs Lionel Lucas presided. The *Jewish Chronicle* reports that:

Cleanliness and tidiness — two virtues which Mrs Lucas is never tired of inculcating in those with whom she is brought into charitable contact — are pervading features of the Department (*JC* 14/3/02).

As a member of the Ladies' Committee of the Jews' Free School, Mrs Lucas was again concerned to influence the appearance of the girls:

> Carrying into Bell Lane the same principles ... , she has toned down a tendency to finery that at one time showed itself among the girls (*JC* ibid).

This 'toning down' of finery could be seen in the context of anti-semitic caricatures insinuating ostentatious dressing by Jewish women.

## *Thrift*

Thrift was another virtue promoted by many of the ladies' philanthropic organisations. Lady visitors were urged to 'encourage working men and women to join thrift societies, to save all that is possible during the busy season''. At Mrs Lucas's Work-Rooms the girls paid into a savings' fund over £100 a year, 'receiving in return a liberal rate of interest'. Another savings plan was offered by the Sick Room Helps Society, which dispensed relief to destitute pregnant women and also served as a Women's Sick Benefit Society. By paying the sum of 10/- by weekly instalments, women gained entitlement to the assistance of a Sick Room Help or Nurse for a period of two weeks. This was seen as a valuable lesson in thrift, saving to provide against future contingencies. The growth of the society to 1,000 members by 1902 was held to indicate that, 'in our Ghetto, with all its complexity of problems and its foreign life on English soil, there is a spirit of independence and self-help which will thrive', if fostered (*JC* 16/5/02, paper by Mrs Model).

The encouragement of thrift was closely related to the desire of the philanthropists to discourage pauperism and promote self-help among the immigrants. Although contemporary non-Jewish workers placed a similar emphasis on the need to teach the poor to stand on their own feet without dependence on charity and to distinguish between cases of feigned and genuine distress, some Anglo-Jewish philanthropists appeared to perceive their working-class co-religionists as particularly prone to reliance on charitable aid. Thus one Conference speaker asserted that, 'our poor people are the greatest, most persistent, most unabashed beggars' (*JC* 23/5/02, Mrs Salis Simon). She attributed this to the immigrants' 'pious and touching belief that an all-wise Providence created poverty on purpose to allow wealth to exercise the cardinal virtue of charity'. While 'centuries of bitter humiliation' had firmly engendered this belief, she believed that: 'it will only take a generation or two of liberty and humanising influence to up-root it and restore our people to self-respect and independence' (ibid).

The philanthropists' concern with the eradication of charitable dependence, as with cleanliness and tidiness, echoed prevailing attitudes to poverty in contemporary English society, but was sharpened by anti-Jewish accusations levelled at the immigrants, and reproduced in the proceedings of the Commission on Alien Immigration. Yet the above conception of the immigrants' propensity to charitable dependence receives little support from interviews conducted with the children of Jewish immigrants. Interviewees repeatedly emphasise the unyielding pride of their parents and their determination to survive without recourse to charity:

> My father died when he was 43 ... My mother was left to struggle through. And she was a very independent woman. She could have got lots of help ... Jewish people had a Benevolent Society and a Board of Guardians ... But she would have sooner that we all starved to death than that she should take anything off anybody. That was her nature.[19]

Rather than turn to charity, immigrant women developed a number of strategies to economise and to survive. They picked over discarded coke cinders for fuel, bought market produce 'either for nothing or for a very nominal sum' at the end of the day; they made up clothes from remnants and tried to provide their families with appetising meals at low cost.[20] Where such economising strategies were not enough to ensure survival, help would be sought through various support mechanisms which existed within the immigrant community: through family networks, neighbours or *landsleit* (immigrants from the same area in Eastern Europe). In an example of neighbourhood assistance probably deriving from Eastern European traditions, a woman who ran a grocery shop would place a basket in the middle of the shop and ask customers to give a gift for charity. Her children would take the basket round the back-streets by night, leaving it anonymously at the house of a family known to be in need.[21]

Although instances of individual acts of support within the immigrant community abound, application was generally only made to formal philanthropic institutions, such as the Jewish Board of Guardians, with extreme reluctance and as a final resort, when a woman's efforts at scrimping and saving and the safety net of mutual aid proved insufficient to meet the extent of a family's crisis. Thus, when a widow with six young children fell ill before her attempt at setting up a small business could reach fruition, and became bed-ridden, her sisters and neighbours helped out with food and cooking, and recourse was made to the pawnbroker. In contrast to the careful anonymity of the shopkeeper's charity, most Anglo-Jewish philanthropic agencies showed little sensitivity to the feelings of those they were assisting. An interviewee remembers vividly his embarrassment when free clothing was distributed:

> They used to do it in front of all the other kids ... They'd call you out, those who er want free shoes ... The other children used to look at you and they would er, they would sort of choose their friends accordingly.[22]

The Jewish Ladies' Clothing Society in Manchester used the distribution of free clothing as an opportunity to exert socialising pressure on the immigrants, making the good behaviour and regular attendance of children at the Jews' School a condition of relief. In this way, the role of the school in socialising and anglicising the children of immigrants was reinforced.[23]

### Good Housewifery

Whereas for boys academic achievement, physical exercise and practical training in skills such as carpentry were stressed, particular attention was directed to the manners and deportment of the girls, and to domestic work and household management. Such training might be given informally, through the advice of the district visitor, but, increasingly, steps were taken to provide formal tuition in domestic skills at institutions established and managed by the philanthropists. By 1902, the Jewish Orphanage at Norwood had its own domestic trainer, teaching 'every branch of home labour': housework, cooking, washing, silver cleaning, needlework and dressmaking, and plans were in motion at the Manchester Jews' School to establish a domestic science flat, where girls in their last year could learn household management, with the intended effect that:

> We shall have in the future young housewives who have been taught practical domestic work ... under easy but thorough discipline. The importance of household duties will be learned, and will make an everlasting impression, as it will be taught at a time when it will be most highly appreciated, and a link thus made between actual school life and outside work (*JC* 25/7/02, paper by Miss Raphael, head-mistress at the Manchester Jews' School.)

Such lessons not only provided a means of improving standards of housewifery in the immigrant community; they also served as an appropriate training for future domestic servants, and considerable effort was in fact directed to the channelling of Jewish girls into domestic service. Thus the Secretary of the Ladies' Committee of Norwood Orphanage considered that the principal work of her committee should be to look after the girls at the institution, 'training as many of them as possible for domestic service'. She attributed the reluctance of Jewish girls to take up this employment to 'the bad influence which their people exercise over them when they leave the institution'. In order to counteract this influence, the Ladies' Committee started to visit the girls' homes, seeking to dissuade parents or relatives from 'interfering with the objects of their training' (*JC* 9/5/02).

Several factors combined to produce this emphasis on domestic service. On one level, the philanthropists were anxious to ease overcrowding in occupations, such as tailoring, where there were particularly high concentrations of Jewish workers — an overcrowding that was given prominence in the reports of the Commission on Alien Immigration. Attempts were therefore made to apprentice girls into millinery and areas unrelated to the tailoring trades, such as the manufacture of electric lighting and lead pencils, upholstery, book-binding, flower-making and purse-making. For the philanthropists, however, domestic service was the preferred alternative, since it represented a 'respectable' occupation, which ensured the girls' supervision in a 'sheltered dwelling' (such as their own). This was deemed particularly important for girls from Norwood Orphanage or the homes established by the Jewish Association for the Protection of Girls and Women.

Equally important was the knowledge that domestic servants were in demand, and nowhere would Jewish servants be more welcome than in the homes of the philanthropists and their peers. One lady philanthropist referred to 'the large and increasing demand for Jewish servants' (*JC* 9/5/02), while the headmistress of the Manchester Jews' School commented on the reluctance of Jewish girls to enter domestic service:

It is a decided loss to our community, that when nursemaids are engaged for our little ones, they should not be Jewesses. Mothers would have far more ease of mind if they could feel they were entrusting their children to competent nurses of their own faith (*JC* 25/7/02).

## *Spiritual Guardian or Material Provider?*

A more subtle and general concern of the lady philanthropists was to communicate to their poorer 'sisters' their own conception of the spiritual and domestic role of women. At the Sabbath Services run by the Jewish Ladies' Visiting Association, the girls

> ... learnt that the future of our race will depend on the goodness of the women, and that while all cannot be clever and beautiful, each one can improve the world by cultivating gentleness, piety, firmness and graciousness. Women may not take an active part in the public functions of our religion, but it is the mother, sister or wife of the man who helps in some way to perform each religious observance (*JC* 25/7/02).

They were taught by the minister that:

> there need be no question of 'Women's Rights'; a girl and a woman will always have them as long as she does her duty well, and remembers that she was created to be the helper of man, to try to encourage him to nobler efforts, and to be ever ready with words and actions of kindness, tenderness and charity. The true woman should be the soul of her home, and if she wants to be happy, should cultivate cheerfulness and make the best of her surroundings, and then she will have neither time nor inclination to think much of the faults of others (ibid).

Although the speaker makes reference to 'the never-failing source of the Scriptures', this conception of women's duties derives more from Evangelical discussions of 'women's mission', which exerted a pervasive influence among the middle classes of nineteenth century England,[24] than from traditional Jewish values. According to Orthodox Judaism, women were largely excluded from the domain of public religion and were traditionally assigned an important role in the home. Yet they were not prevented from engaging in secular activities outside the home, nor were they depicted as essentially spiritual in nature. The 'woman of worth' described in the Book of Proverbs is active and resourceful; while her concern is to 'do her husband good', it is in practical and material ways (*Proverbs* xxxi 10-3).

In the traditional Eastern European communities from which many of the immigrants came, a key distinction was drawn between the spheres of the sacred — associated with men and their activities of religious scholarship and prayer — and the profane — associated with women. An opposition was drawn not between the workplace and the home but between the synagogue or study-house and the home, which was perceived as the locus of profane, material activities, which often included breadwinning. As in 19th century England, women were seen primarily as homemakers, but they often also assumed the role of material providers so their husbands could devote more time to the esteemed sphere of religion.[25] Either way, women were not permitted to play an active role in public religion and had to be content with an enabling role for their menfolk. However, the contrast between Jewish women's role in the two communities was sharp. In Eastern Europe, her role was that of material provider, in England that of spiritual helpmeet.

In their emphasis on women's role within the domestic environment, the lady philanthropists supported and reinforced the informal pressures of British society. The immigrant women were encouraged to remain at home after marriage and to improve their standards of housewifery. In her preliminary address, the Conference President described how charitable workers should:

> encourage girls to put into practice at home the knowledge of cooking, sewing and domestic economy acquired at school. In short, they can help to make better housewives ... (*JC* 16/5/02).

Although close reference was generally made to the Charity Organisation Society, in certain cases the Anglo-Jewish ladies stressed instead women's domesticity, even at the expense of the cherished principle of self-help. Thus Miss Hannah Hyam asserted that, while she agreed with the guiding principle of the COS that a mother should be made to feel responsible for the welfare of her children,

> sending women with young families out to work except in special cases, I am very much opposed to; it is the cause of the ruin of many young lives (*JC* 30/5/02).

She therefore recommended that, where a woman with a young family had been widowed she should be given charitable assistance in the form of 'a fixed weekly allowance on a rather liberal scale', rather than be forced to go out to work.

The effectiveness of the pressures on working-class Jewish women towards a more exclusive domestic orientation is demonstrated by a comparison of the economic activities of first and second generation immigrants. An analysis of 150 oral history interviews conducted with the children of Jewish immigrants in Manchester, indicates a sharp decrease in the number of Jewish women who assumed an active breadwinning role after marriage, among the second generation. Whereas about two-thirds of the mothers of interviewees had engaged in some form of economic activity after the birth of their children, only 38% of married women of the interviewee generation took on paid work after marriage.[26]

This trend is confirmed by informants, who recall that:

> In those days, not the rule but the custom was — a girl got married — a Jewish girl got married — it was her duty to stay at home and look after her home and husband, and have his meal ready, and a nice, clean home and a fire to come home to ... Those days, a man was king in his castle ... It was a very rare thing for a Jewish girl to get married and go out to work.[27]

Other informants emphasise the stigma attached to working after marriage:

> It wasn't done in those days. Before you got married, you left work two weeks before and I've never been back to work since, never. And I wish I could have done then, because I would have earned more than my husband earned, but you didn't do it, it was just not done, it wasn't the thing ... you'd rather starve and not go ... that was the *yichus* (status) in those days, which I think is a terrible thing.[28]

This interviewee's insistence on not working is particularly striking, in view of her own mother's career as a credit draper and her grandmother's as the keeper of a wayside inn and leather shop in Galicia.

### The relationship between the philanthropists and the immigrant women

The contact between Jewish child and philanthropist, begun early in life through the visits of the School Manager and District Visitor, and intensified during school days, was not lost once the girl left school. The philanthropists kept in touch with the girls. One way of doing so was for the School Manager to build up a close relationship with the girl in her last year at school, and to try to guide her into an appropriate occupation, ensuring that the lessons of punctuality, regularity and industry were not negated by a period of unemployment between work and school. At Norwood, each girl was assigned a member of the Ladies' Committee as a 'guardian and friend', to whom she became 'an object of individual attention' (*JC* 9/5/02). The Ladies' Committee kept a Case Book with 'full particulars' of each girl during her last six months at Norwood and when she left her name was transferred to another book, where her development over the next three years was recorded.

A second method was to set up 'Old Scholars' Guilds' and Girls' Clubs to link the girls' school life with their working life and to provide School Managers with a way of maintaining contact with their former pupils. Jewish women were in the forefront of the development of such clubs. Lily Montagu, who established the West Central Girls' Club in London, was a founder member of the National Organisation of Girls' Clubs and gave talks all over the country on the role of girls' clubs and the meaning of club membership. Such clubs might offer recreational facilities (for example ping-pong, dancing, chess and dominoes), entertainments, such as lectures and lantern-slides, as well as instruction on topics such as 'wise expenditure in regard to dress', and further educational opportunities.

The desire of the club leaders to bring 'some measure of culture and comfort into the lives of our working girls' (*JC* 16/5/02) was underpinned by the desire to keep Jewish girls off the streets. According to the *Jewish Chronicle*, the clubs were founded as a result of recognition by communal workers that:

> the class of girls for whom the clubs are established would, under no circumstances, be satisfied to spend their evenings at home, in rooms which offer the scantiest accommodation, and that the club-room, in the circumstances, is the safest refuge from the streets (JC 14/3/02).

This concern with the prevention of prostitution reflected a general preoccupation among Victorian women philanthropists. Prochaska describes ladies pursuing active rescue work at factory gates, dockyard dining-halls, with needlewomen in sweatshops and with navvies at their encampments:

> As guardians of the home and of the purity of family life they defended 'the very fountains of the national life'.[29]

Jewish women were aware of the interest shown by bodies such as the Commission on Alien Immigration over the extent of Jewish prostitution, and of the prominence given to cases involving Jewish prostitutes or procurers by men like Major Evans-Gordon, who sought to demonstrate the polluting effect of Jewish immigration upon English society. While members of the Jewish Association for the Protection of Girls and Women directed their attention to active rescue and preventive work, the provision of girls' clubs was seen as making a complementary contribution to the prevention of Jewish prostitution:

> It is impossible for a strong association of women workers to escape from contact with certain forms of vice, though we pin our faith more on prevention and try to establish a strong hold on our young sisters by our Girls' Clubs and Sabbath Services (*JC* 23/5/02).

A recruit to the Girls' Club recalled that its purpose was 'to keep us pure and holy ... even now I don't know what the aim was, except to take us off the street and to give us a bit of culture.'[30]

While the Anglo-Jewish lady philanthropists saw themselves as providing a model for the immigrant women and their daughters, in practice a near impenetrable class gulf separated the women of the two communities, and any similarities in their lifestyle and expectations were extremely limited. Class differences over-rode religious communalities, and the Anglo-Jewish ladies did not regard the immigrants as their social equals. They sought to instil in the women of the immigrant community English notions of femininity, and at the same time to socialise them into the 'respectable ' working classes.

To the extent to which the philanthropists were successful in communicating their vision of the Jewish woman's role, they served to place a brake on the autonomy of Jewish women within the immigrant community. Whereas in Eastern Europe the Jewish woman's role as material provider gave her considerable scope for initiative and independent action, even if she enjoyed no formal status in the religious sphere, the logic implicit in the philanthropists' policies was to restrict her role outside the home, while still not admitting her to a full participation in Jewish religious life.[31] Evidence also suggests that the limitation of her autonomy in this way had the effect of undermining her authority within the home, since in economic as well as religious matters she became increasingly dependent on her husband.[32]

Paradoxically, while perhaps inadvertently undermining the authority of Jewish women within the immigrant community, the Anglo-Jewish ladies were simultaneously extending their own scope for independent action, through their very involvement in charitable work. For these women, as for middle-class women more generally,[33] philanthropy played an important role in securing for women a sphere of independent action outside the immediate domestic environment. By 1902, middle class women of the Anglo-Jewish community enjoyed a greater degree of personal freedom than in the preceding half-century, and they were also beginning to secure a degree of representation in communal affairs. A small number of lady representatives now sat on the general committees of the London Jewish Board of Guardians, the Jews' Infant School and the Jews' Hospital and Orphan Asylum at Norwood, all of which had hitherto been entirely male preserves. In the case of Norwood this representation was secured in the face of 'tremendous' opposition, but the result proved so successful that:

> those who at the outset were most bitterly opposed to it are now loudest in its praises, while gentlemen often ask the ladies to under-take duties which formerly they thought they alone were competent to perform (*JC* 9/5/02).

## Conclusion

Few of the lady philanthropists in 1902 would have openly expressed a dissatisfaction with the existing order of gender relations, or acknowledged sympathy with the more radical aims of the contemporary Women's Rights and Suffrage Movement. Most of the papers presented at the Conference of Jewish Women affirmed an acceptance of the existing division of labour and of prevailing definitions of the Jewish woman's role. Yet, through their involvement in philanthropic work, the women were gaining confidence and organisational experience; they were forging links with other women, Jewish and non-Jewish, pursuing charitable work outside the home; and their growing awareness of their own latent abilities and the useful purposes to which these might be directed was leading them to make demands on hitherto unquestioned male restrictions. However uncontentious the claims of the conference organisers, the very holding of such an event, gathering together Jewish women from all over the country, had significance for women's consciousness. It was a public statement of their achievements in a sphere outside the domestic environ-ment, and it expressed for the first time a sense of unity and solidarity among Jewish women nation-wide, given tangible form in the Union of Jewish Women, established as a result of the Conference 'to promote the social, moral and spiritual welfare of Jewish women, and to induce practical cooperation between Jewish women workers throughout the country'. Although political demands were not made at this stage, a feminist consciousness was rising: several of the women who figured prominently at the Conference later became active in the Jewish League for Women's Suffrage (established 1912) and the Society for the Amelioration of the Legal Position of the Jewess.

In 1902, Jewish women of the immigrant community and the Anglo-Jewish middle classes were to some extent moving in opposite directions. For the immigrant women and their daughters, the pressures received, both from the wider society and from the Anglo-Jewish establishment through the agency of the lady philanthropists and their institutions, were to a more exclusively domestic orientation, with decreasing participation in secular life outside the home; a shift from material provider to housewife and spiritual helpmeet. Philanthropy afforded middle-class women of the Anglo-Jewish community a degree of autonomy, a means of pursuing independent activities outside the home, and of making an active contribution to communal life, so extending their role from spiritual helpmeet to communal worker. Yet the irony in the concomitant development of these two related trajectories would not have been easily apparent at the time. For the philanthropists continued to uphold and project the ideal of the English Jewish woman as domesticated and socially and financial dependent upon her husband. Their philanthropic work did not entail breadwinning, and their employment of domestic servants — an occupation which they recommended so highly to the daughters of the Jewish poor — enabled them to engage in their outside activities without failing to fulfil their domestic obligations.

## Acknowledgements

I should like to thank Judith Emanuel, Rosalyn Livshin, Lara Marks, Daniel Miller, Sheila Saunders and Bill Williams for their help and comments.

## Notes

1. See R. Burman, 'The Jewish Woman as Breadwinner: The Changing Value of Women's Work in a Manchester Immigrant Community', *Oral History*, 10:2 (1982), pp.27-39; "She Looketh Well to the Ways of Her Household': The Changing Role of Jewish Women in Religious Life c.1880-1930' in G. Malmgreen (ed.), *Religion in the Lives of English Women, 1760-1930* (London, 1986), pp. 234-259 and 'Jewish Women and the Household Economy in Manchester, c.1890-1920' in D.Cesarani (ed.), *The Making of Modern Anglo-Jewry* (Oxford, 1990), pp.55-75. Also L. Marks, "Dear Old Mother Levy's': The Jewish Maternity Home and Sick Room Helps Society 1895-1939', *Social History of Medicine*, 3:1 (April 1990) pp.61-88, 'The Marginalized Heritage of Jewish Women in Britain' in T. Kushner (ed.), *The Jewish Heritage in British History: Englishness and Jewishness* (London, 1992), and *Model*

*Mothers: Jewish Mothers and Maternity Provision in East London 1870-1939* (Oxford, 1994); and L. Gordon Kuzmack, *Woman's Cause: The Jewish Woman's Movement in England and the United States, 1881-1933* (Columbus, Ohio, 1990).

2. These interviews, carried out by the Manchester Studies Unit, Manchester Polytechnic, are now available at the Manchester Jewish Museum. Each interview has been given a number, preceded by 'J', and this will be cited below.

3. See C. Bermant, *The Cousinhood: The Anglo-Jewish Gentry* (London, 1971); V.D. Lipman 'The Age of Emancipation 1815-1880', in V.D. Lipman (ed.) *Three Centuries of Anglo-Jewish History* (Cambridge, 1961); and B. Williams, *The Making of Manchester Jewry 1740-1875* (Manchester, 1976).

4. See V.D. Lipman, *A Social History of the Jews of England 1850-1950* (London, 1954) and L. Gartner, *The Jewish Immigrant in England 1870-1914* (London, 1960).

5. Gordon Kuzmack op. cit., p.12.

6. V.D. Lipman, *A Century of Social Service: A History of the Jewish Board of Guardians 1859-1959* (London 1959), p.114-116.

7. See L. Marks, 'The Experience of Jewish Prostitutes and Jewish Women in the East End of London at the Turn of the Century', *The Jewish Quarterly* 34:2 (1987) and "The Luckless Waifs and Strays of Humanity': Irish and Jewish Immigrant Unwed Mothers in London 1870-1939', *Twentieth Century British History* 3:2 (1992), pp.113- 137.

8. Interview J128.

9. A term used by interviewee J15.

10. Manchester JLVA 25th Annual Report, *Retrospect of 25 Years' Work,* p.6.

11. See L. Davidoff and C. Hall, *Family Fortunes: Men and Women of the English Middle Classes 1780-1850* (London 1987).

12. *ibid.*, p. 149.

13. An article in The Jewish World (19 September 1902) notes that before the Conference, some of its critics freely stated that it would result in nothing but 'tea parties and talk'. However, it admits that the 'self-complimentary fiction' that women were impractical had 'received a series of knockdown blows' as a result of the successful organisation of the Conference.

14. F. K. Prochaska, *Women and Philanthropy in 19th Century England* (Oxford, 1980) and L. Davidoff and C. Hall, op.cit.

15. Prochaska op. cit., pp.5-11 and 117-125.

16. *ibid.*, p.98.

17. Interview J143.

18. JLVA Annual Reports, Manchester Central Archives.

19. Interview J279.

20. R. Burman (1990), pp.66-69.

21. Interview J273.

22. *ibid.*

23. For further details of the pressure exerted by the Jewish Ladies' Clothing Society and a more general examination of the role of the Jews' School in anglicising the children of immigrants, see R. Livshin, 'Aspects of the Acculturation of the Children of Immigrant Jews in Manchester 1890-1930' (M.Ed thesis, University of Manchester 1982).

24. See C. Hall 'The Early Formation of the Victorian Domestic Ideology' in S. Burman (ed.) *Fit Work for Women* (London, 1979), pp.15-32.

25. R. Burman (1982), pp. 27-39.
26. R. Burman (1990), pp. 55-75.
27. Interview J66.
28. Interview J104.
29. Prochaska, op. cit., p.184. For discussions of Jewish prostitution and rescue work, see L. Marks (1987) and E.J. Bristow, *Vice and Vigilance* (London, 1977).
30. Interview J287.
31. R. Burman (1986), pp. 252-253.
32. R. Burman, 1990, pp. 71-72.
33. Prochaska, op. cit.

## References

Burman, R. 1982 'The Jewish Woman as Breadwinner: The Changing Value of Women's Work in a Manchester Immigrant Community', *Oral History* 10:2, pp. 27-39.

Burman, R. 1984 'Growing up in Manchester Jewry — The Story of Clara Weingard', *Oral History* 12:1, pp. 56-63.

Burman, R. 1986 'She Looketh Well to the Ways of Her Household': The Changing Role of Jewish Women in Religious Life c.1880-1930' in G. Malmgreen (ed.), *Religion in the Lives of English Women, 1760-1930* (London), pp. 234-259.

Burman, R. 1990 'Jewish Women and the Household Economy in Manchester, c.1890-1920' in D. Cesarani (ed.) *The Making of Modern Anglo-Jewry* (Oxford), pp. 55-75.

Gordon Kuzmack, L. 1990 *Woman's Cause: The Jewish Woman's Movement in England and the United States, 1881-1933* (Columbus, Ohio).

Jewish Women in London Group 1989 *Generations of Memories: Voices of Jewish Women* (London).

Manchester Jewish Museum 1992 *Women of Worth: Jewish Women in Britain* (catalogue to accompany exhibition).

Marks, L. 1987 'The Experience of Jewish Prostitutes and Jewish Women in the East End of London at the Turn of the Century', *The Jewish Quarterly* 34:2, pp. 6-10.

Marks, L. 1992a 'The Luckless Waifs and Strays of Humanity: Irish and Jewish Immigrant Unwed Mothers in London 1870-1939', *Twentieth Century British History* 3:2, pp. 113-137.

Marks, L. 1992b 'The Marginalised Heritage of Jewish Women in Britain' in T. Kushner (ed.), *The Jewish Heritage in British History: Englishness and Jewishness* (London), pp. 106-127.

Marks, L. 1994 *Model Mothers — Jewish Mothers and Maternity Provision in East London 1870-1939* (Oxford).

Prochaska, F.K. 1980 *Women and Philanthropy in l9th Century England* (Oxford).

# Index